Life Reflections

by

Alice Laura Hartley

First published by AuthorHouse 05/12/05

ISBN: 1-4208-3002-3 (sc)

Printed in the United States of America
Bloomington, Indiana

This book is printed on acid-free paper.

author HOUSE

1663 LIBERTY DRIVE
BLOOMINGTON, INDIANA 47403
(800) 839-8640
www.authorhouse.com

SPECIAL THANKS

I would like to specially thank all my family in helping me compile this book. When I started I had no knowledge of a Computer and my typing is hunt and peck. Some of the spelling and typing errors are mine and some are the way Aunt Alice had them written. I didn't want to take away from her spelling and the meaning intended.

Also I would like to thank Daryl Dille and his help in starting me on the Computer.

A special thanks to my Granddaughter, Deserae Allred Orton, for her design of the Front and Back Cover of the book.

This was my Aunt's last desire, to have her book published. It has been a deep emotional experience and a special privilege.

Sue Carrol Henrikson Ward, Niece

TABLE OF CONTENTS

HISTORY WRITTEN BY ALICE LAURA HENRIKSON HARTLEY

Zooming in on 8 decades on this earth sounds like a long time. The one comforting thing is each decade is exciting. I was born June 15, 1907 at Rockville, Nebraska. My parents were Ida Mary Gray Henrikson and Frank Oscar C. Henrikson. Some of my Mother's people were Pennsylvania Dutch, also some settled in Tennessee. Our Mother was born in Sydney, Iowa. Our Father was born in Sweden. He moved to the U.S.A. when he was 12 years old. His folks settled in Boelus, Nebraska. Just before the turn of the century found my folks homesteading in Idaho. Grandpa Gray settled there too. His children, Herby, Bert, F., Stella and Roy, settled in Idaho too. Grandpa was a widower and later married Maud Bishop. Their son Alfred is in Oregon at this time.

After the turn of the century Frank and Ida Henrikson moved back to Nebraska and farmed until we lost our Mother in 1915. In 1918 we moved to Canada. Dad took up a Homestead. Our family consisted of Jennie, Orah, Mae, Eda, Earl and myself, Alice. Orah didn't go with us to Canada, she was married to Melvin Sickels.

Jennie was married to Alfred Minshull, but they went to Canada with us. They had 4 children, Ida, Marie, John, Beulah. Alberta, Evelyn, and Alfred Jr. were born in Canada. They moved back to Idaho with Earl and I in 1926 with Grandpa Gray. We came to New Plymouth. Payette was a close town and we found work there. Being in Canada we were short of fruit. It was a thrill to have such a plenty. Jennie canned that fall, what an abundance! Lucky she did, it was such a shortage of work for Alfred and Earl. I had a job as salad girl in a hotel. The boss let me bring food home that was perishable for the family. They had to wait until around 8:30 every night to eat dinner. Earl was hurt on the Egyptian theater that fall in Boise, so he was unable to work.

The Minshulls moved to Boise in 1927. Work opened up for both Earl and Alfred. I stayed in Payette and later moved to Weiser. I was in café work. I bought my first piano, Gulbransen, brand new. I married Lee Holloway September 27, 1928. Earl married Gwen Burch that fall, too. Well the depression moved in on us. We decided to take off for California. Myrtle Smith and Ed Roubough were friends. So we 3 couples took off Thanksgiving day. We got as far as Wells, Nevada and enjoyed our dinner with snow spitting in our face . Still singing "Big Rock Candy Mountain" we made it to Reno. First night, we could only afford one cabin. I think around $1.00 a night. Next day we started up over Donner Pass. A big sign was posted, "Travel at your own risk." We paid no attention. Well, snow and more snow. Halfway, more or less, Earl was in a Sports Car [Nash] with wire wheels and one broke down. He had a spare wheel. Not all the spokes were there, so the men folk replaced 27 spokes. The women tried to start a fire. Lucky for us a little black lady visited us before we left Boise and reminded us to have magazines with us to encourage a fire to start with wet wood. Sure enough, it helped and we got pots out and cooked a hot meal.

Darkness was over taking us, soon the roads would be closed in. Still with determination we started on slippery roads. Sliding almost over the canyon. Gwen was so frightened. We sat in the back seat and I covered her head and stretched the truth and said "The roads weren't bad and everything is O.K." Lee stood on the running board and scraped the windshields as Earl drove. Ed and Myrtle toughed it out in back of us. When I first saw the lights of some homes, we were coming down into a valley. It was rain instead of snow. Our prayers were answered.

We soon found a cabin, but they wouldn't rent to three couples. We hide one couple, as it was dark. When the landlord went in, we all moved in. It was only $1.00. The next morning California looked like Spring. We did check on the roads we came over, it was posted "closed for the winter". The Big Rock Candy Mountain song danced in our heads. Now looking for work was the next step. Orange groves were a plenty, so we hired out. In a few days I got a job in a restaurant. The rest of the group worked in oranges and olives. That played out, Gwen and I went into a bingo game and made some extra money.

Then we started on south. The farther south, the tougher it got. In Redding, California, I got another job in a high class restaurant.

For banquets I had to dress in black. They furnished the cap and apron. They didn't hire transit, so I told them I was a native. By then we lived close to a garbage dump. We had an auto tent that belonged to Ed. That meant Gwen, Earl, Lee and I had a bed spread and stretched it over our beds. Well to get me ready for work was something. Our stove was a smudge pot. It wasn't bad to cook on. We ironed my black dress by wrapping it around the stove. I was inspected by the crew to see if I had soot on me before I took off for work. I finally got enough to buy orange sacks so the men folk could go to work. They worked one day, no way of making any thing. In the mean time it rained and my clothes were soaked. No way could I report for work. God smiled on us, the boys got a job on the San Bernardino Dam. Was good money. Close to us they were dumping oranges by the truck load as the prices didn't suit them. So the oranges were destroyed. I shall never forget the aroma. Every one in the camp enjoyed them.

Gwen and I got some car seats and made us a softer bed. In two weeks the job was over, so we took off for Long Beach. We had a cabin on the ocean. We enjoyed the beach, digging clams, abalones and crab. We decided to cook the crabs in the cabin, wrong thing to do. We almost had to move out the odor was terrific!

The men got work in a raw fish factory. Their clothes weren't allowed in the house. We met them at the door and they had to shower and dress in the rest rooms. Wash day came, Earl and I went to see what we could do with soap, lye, we tried it all. When Earl finished his woolen pants, the holes were too much, so to the trash for them.

We had beautiful shells drying on the roof of our cabin. We looked one day and they were gone, but scattered on another roof drying. So Ed and I went and got them back. We had all of them named and claimed. The ones in the cabin didn't peep. They were pretty tough and good sized.

I got a job in a restaurant as a single person, she didn't hire married people. It didn't take long for my husband to ruin that job. Gwen and I worked in the tuna. It was a nice clean job. Spring was in the making, Ed, Myrtle, Lee and I started north. We stopped in Bakersfield and the men got work. Myrtle and I took it easy for 2 weeks, then on to Sacramento. The spinach was being harvested and we all got jobs in the canneries. Earl and Gwen were still in Long Beach. Gwen's Father sent her a ticket for the train and Earl had a broken down car. He scrambled around and found parts for the car and started towards Sacramento. He said he knew if he got there his sister would find room for him. He was on an almost empty tank. He picked up 2 hitch hikers and told them they could ride until the gas ran out. They filled his tank and put them right into Sacramento. He was a painter and found work to get the money to go back to Boise, Idaho. That November 15, 1929, Sue Carrol Henrikson was born.

Lee and I got enough money to buy a car, an Elgin, with spinach money to go to Alturas, California. We took a fence post project. Not long we found rattle snakes were thick. Sleeping in a tent was scary. I was cooking for 5 men on a campfire. Lizards were jumping from rock to rock. We had to watch every minute for snakes. We could hear the cougars yell every night. The moon light shining on the rocks was a pretty sight. We took off and went to Hood River, Oregon and worked in the strawberries. Most beautiful berries I ever saw. The end of the season we went to Olympia, Washington. We visited Jennie, Alfred and family and then came back to Payette, Idaho. The trip was exciting, uncertain, but experience was no name for it.

Gwen had a $2.50 gold piece we would pond for food. Then get some money and regain it. The strip on the ocean front was a high light. The smell of the hamburgers were out of this world. We didn't always have the money to buy one.

Surely God traveled with us. We were never hungry. Myrtle and I didn't have nylons or hose. Gwen was lucky, her folks sent her some from time to time. One day Gwen and I walked 4 miles in Long Beach to get the mail. Eda had sent us a Christmas Cake, that could have been February when we got it. Being a fruit cake, it kept good.

When depression started, it subsided, I was single and in 1936 married Dee Hartley. I was teaching music and we bought a one roomed shack. Shortly after we were married, in a years time, we had a new home built. Dee and I were playing in night clubs and dances. Earl and Gwen raised a nice family, Sue Carrol, Alice, Carl and Anita. Earl followed the mechanic work and passed away in April 1972. Gwen has had a child care for many a year and has been loyal to her church services for music and accompanying different functions.

Music has been a big part in my life. Group, private lessons, and orchestra work. I've taught group dramatics and vocal work. I was hired by the Woodman of the World for 20 years, as well as other projects too.

This is my 50th year teaching. I am a widow now, Dee passed away May 18, 1985. I am compiling a book with plays, poems, song poems, along with cooking, painting and sewing. In order to stay in the business it took a lot of study. I cooked for groups with 40 to 125 in the group. A recital called for costumes, props for the stage to be painted. My plays were original. We had T.V. skits and radio programs. Eda and I are the only ones left of our family now. I have a lot of nice nieces and nephews to be thankful for. Last but not least, my grand nieces and nephews are very dear to me.

RAMBLING AT RANDOM WITH BITS AND PIECES

Where did I come into the Gray family? William Alfred Gray was my grandfather. And a grand old man was he. He was so kind to everyone. He stood tall and stately, with love to go around to the family, never slighted any of us. He fought in the Civil War.

My Mother, Ida Mary Gray was the eldest in the family of his second marriage. They lost their Mother when she was quite young. Ida took over the duties helping to raise the family. The youngest, Roy, was her pride and joy. When Ida married Frank Oscar Henrikson, Roy lived with them for a while. Then later Grandpa Gray moved to Idaho from Nebraska. Mom and Dad went to Idaho before the turn of the century, then back to Nebraska.

When I was five years old my Moyher and I took a trip out to Pocatello, Idaho. Uncle Roy and Aunt Daisy were expecting a baby, Adenalo, I believe they called her. She didn't live very long. Of course, Bertha was around, two years old. She was as sharp as a tack, but didn't want to walk on her chicken pox [it hurt]. I walked her anyway, in a few days she was running everywhere.

Mother and I went up to Lost River to visit the rest of the family. Grandpa Gray, Aunt Stella, Uncle F. , Uncle Herby and their families. It was snowing that day and they met us at the train with bob sleigh and cutters. They looked like Santa's sleigh. By the way, I saw Santa in Pocatello, so that reassured me there really was a Santa.

That was the last trip My Mother had, she died in 1915. What a blow to our family, leaving two married daughters, Jennie and Orah, and four at home, Mae, Eda, Earl and me, Alice.

What a struggle, Mae was fourteen. We expected her to know all the answers. Believe me she tried. Oh, what I would have given to ask mamma how to do things. No bakery bread, no washing machine, no electricity. Our Father was born in Sweden and he knew plenty of hardships. One time in Sweden there was a boat frozen in the ice with there provisions on it. They had to make bread out of tree bark until the ice got safe enough to get their food.

In 1919 Grandpa Hawthorn, Aunt Daisy's Father, came to visit us in Nebraska. We were having one of those Nebraska blizzards, cold, windy, miserable. That fell into a persuasion to talk our Father into going to Canada and take up a homestead. Jennie and her husband, Alfred Minshull, liked the idea too. So we had a big sale, took all the furniture out in the yard, served a lunch, people came for miles around. We cried when we saw all our beautiful furniture hauled away, a piece at a time. By March 27th we were ready to leave. Jennie and Alfred with their 4 children, Ida, Marie, John and Beulah. It was the first time I ever slept in a berth on a train. We carried a lot of food, to cut down on expenses. We were loaded so heavy, everyone had a bag to carry. We, my sisters and I, had our spring hats and coats on, as Spring was in the making when we left. Our first shock was when we woke up in Canada, it was a big snow storm. We traveled several days when we got to Vegaville, Alberta. Uncle Roy was there to meet us.

Winter was trying to break up, so he brought the wagon. The roads were something to behold, chunks of frozen snow a good two feet high, mud in spots and water running every where. We had fifty miles to go. The first night we stopped on an Indian reserve. They let us sleep in their living room of the Indian Chief's residence. We stretched out on the floor. There wasn't anything in the room except a side board, we call a buffet. No chairs, they had benches in the dining room. The next night we stayed at a French hotel with outdoor plumbing. They had them built up to the second floor, so we wouldn't have to go down stairs.

The third day we arrived at Uncle Roy's and Aunt Daisy's. Bertha was so glad to see us. Aileen was just a baby. She was beautiful, long sweeping eye lashes. They had an Indian cook over one hundred years old. She served us baked white fish and bannock. [bannock is flour, salt and water mixed and baked in a slow oven] Sounds strange, but it was good.

In a few days things started popping. They got logs out for our cabin. They had a building bee. Neighbors came from miles around. It was roughed in, in a few hours and we moved in. Of course it wasn't chinked in yet, but that was done in the spare time. By fall we had the chinks mudded in and the shingles on the roof. So many of the homesteaders had dirt roofs.

Uncle Roy and my Father went out and bought a herd of cattle and saddle horses. So that meant we had to herd them. A new experience indeed. Such heavy bush country, it was easy to get lost, but Bertha knew her way around, so she saved us every time.

We enjoyed the wild fruit; such as wild strawberries, saskatoons, currents, high bush cranberries and low bush too. Blue berries, used to have some hill sides just blue with blue berries.

Our little post office was named Boyne Lake. Indians called the lake Floating Stone Lake. Our home was on the lake four and one half miles from school. A long ride on horse back every day with such severe weather.

We had our fun in the snow sleighing, skating, going to dances, in fact our family played for the dances. Waltzing, fox-trots, polkas, murzakas, square dancing and many more.

In our home we never had a Christmas tree or a turkey, but other wild game, such as ; partridges, geese, ducks, moose and deer meat. In the summer we fished every day, so the fish would be fresh, no refrigeration. We had white fish, pickerel, wall eyed pike, perch and some lake trout, not in our lake but farther north. Some of the fish weighed from 3 ½ to 8 or 9 pounds.

In 1920 Mae and Eda were married. Mae married George Martin and Eda married Johnny McDonald. That left me, Alice, chief cook and bottle washer. I was 12 years old. Dad was back with trial and error with a new cook. Baking light bread and scrubbing soft pine floors was quite a task, but I loved it, cause I love to be my own boss. I was deep into music and worked every spare moment on the organ. When Dad was gone I practiced the violin [he forbade me to do] that was his instrument. I played his cello in the case. I wasn't big enough to take it out and get it back. I called them to dinner with my brother's trumpet. Earl was unhappy about that too.

By 1922 our relatives were starting to leave their homesteads. Uncle Roy being a railroad man from Pocatello, Idaho, he had no trouble working part time out of Edmonton, Mirror and Jasper, Alberta, Canada. That kept the expenses going. I looked forward to him coming home in the early spring to work the farm. He never forgot us with gifts, sometimes dresses, I thought they were beautiful. When the family broke up, they left the homestead.

Finely it was just Dad and me left. I took great pride in making soap.

It took   6 lbs. fat or cracklins
1 [13 ounce] can lye
5 cups cold water [soft]
2 tablespoons borax

Mix in a cold iron kettle until dissolved. Cook on a real low heat. Cool and cut into bars.
Then came the flies:
Sticky fly paper: 1 lb. rosin
3 ½ oz. molasses
3 ½ oz. boiled linseed oil

Boil until thick and spread on the paper. Lay it somewhere and wait for the flies. The only trouble, you could always plan on getting stuck in it yourself, or the dog or cat. It did catch flies.

I was always amazed at Grandpa Hawthorne's stories. He fought in the southern civil war. Grandpa being a northern soldier made for a few disagreements. Grandpa Hawthorne told about a battle where he hide behind a tree and forgot to hide his hand. So the enemy shot right through it. He sang from morning 'till night. He loved to be left with the children so he could tell stories and sing. "Golden Slippers" was one of his favorites.

I left the homestead when I was 16 years old and went to Calgary to work. Jennie, Alfred, Eda and Johnny and families were already there. Earl and I worked out of Calgary until 1926. Grandpa Gray, his wife, Maud, and son, Alfred made a trip to Calgary and Jennie's family, Earl and me [Alice] started back to Idaho with them. At the Canadian line, we were informed that the Canadian children, Alberta, Evelyn, and Alfred Jr. had to pay a head tax. That broke Earl and I right there, as Jennie and Alfred had only enough gas money to get us where we were going. In Colfax Washington, we had a big break down. It took a week to repair Alfred's car. Grandpa was driving a new model T Ford. Of course he bailed us out and bought food and gas. We camped out with a holy tent, it was more holy than righteous, or course we were lucky it didn't rain.

After two weeks on the road we landed in New Plymouth, Idaho. Grandpa had a little acreage there. I called it the Garden of Eden, beautiful fruit and vegetables. Believe me we were ready for that kind of food after 7 years in Canada. I told Grandpa I plan to own property in Idaho and settle here. What a sad day for our Christmas of 1926, Grandpa Gray dropped dead of a heart attack at the age of 79 years.

Nineteen twenty seven was a tough time for everyone. Alfred with their seven children, Ida, Marie, John, Beulah, Alberta, Evelyn and Alfred Jr. Shortly after New Years little Evelyn passed away with pneumonia. Work was scarce. I had a job in a hotel as salad girl. The boss knew we were in need of food for the family so she gave me leftovers to take home. They had to wait until about 8:30 every night for their supper. Jennie had canned lots of fruit in the summer and that was a God's send. In the spring Alfred went back to work.

Depression in full swing that year and the next few years. Even with bread 5 cents a loaf, hamburger 10 cents a pound, dress material as low as 5 cents a yard. We still didn't have enough to buy freely. A lot of people went to the deserts and gathered sage brush to heat the house and cook with. One could buy an acre for as low as 500 dollars, with a very low payment, maybe $15 or $25 per month.

We tried to get ahold of all the old antiques we could, such as; Old muzzle loading guns, treadle sewing machines, coffee grinders, and old phonographs. Uncle Roy had a disk phonograph. [That would be a prize now]

Aunt Stella, that lived on Lost River [a little town called Darlington], was such a dear person. She passed away in 1968. She stayed in her log house with the dirt roof until she died. The Mormons would have liked to claim her as one of them, but she rebelled, although they gave her a Mormon funeral. They spoke of her as being a mid-wife, she helped deliver 600 babies, more or less. Sometimes there was a Dr. present and sometimes not. They owned a cattle ranch. Uncle Lou Evans passed away before she did. There were three sons, Arthur, Melvin and Milfred, known as Babe.

Uncle Roy's eldest brother, Herby, lived on Lost River too. He married Ada Evans, Uncle Lou's sister. He was a wonderful manager, very shrewd when it came to dealing. That was a Gray trait all down through the family. Some of the Grays were good horse traders and run horse races. Uncle Herby and Aunt Ada had one daughter, Sarah. She taught school all of her working life. At this time, 1977, she lives at Moses Lake, Washington.

Uncle F. was quite a traveler. He started on Lost River, then went to Canada to homestead, then to New York state and raised a family, Harold, Donald, Harvey, Bert, John and Hannah. Aunt Jean was not too strong. She passed away in the fifties and he remarried. Aunt Myrtle is still alive. She took such good care of him at the last. He died in the early seventy's. He came back to Idaho in the 30's. Farmed awhile at New Plymouth, Idaho.

In the early forty's money was more plentiful, lots of work. For those who wanted to get ahead could. My husband, Dee Hartley, was mixed up in real estate, which turned out to our advantage. Dee worked with heavy equipment, that took him all over the state. That meant mountain camps, trailer houses. He built lots of secondary roads in the mountains that are still in use.

We have a summer home now in Cascade, Idaho. We go up in the summer on the week-ends and fish. We did have a boat. We are close to the Cascade Lake.

LOOKING BACK WITH A SMILE
The unforgettable dinner

I was a September bride in 1928. We rented a place with huge old walnut trees. We spent the autumn days gathering the nuts and hulling them to store for winter.

Where we lived in Idaho, it was a nice drive into the mountains. We gathered such pretty leaves, mountain ash berries, they are so red and pretty.

It's always a challenge to meet the in-laws. I fell in love with Mom and Dad. When I first came into the family, I was so anxious to show them I could cook. The date was set. I always set the table early to devote time to the last minute details.

First a table decoration was a must. With a pretty piece of drift wood, I arranged the colorful leaves, mountain ash berries and even added a few herb leaves for aroma. Well that was ready.

Our only table cloth was laundered and starched crisp and nice. Of course new table settings, I was so proud.

I knew I had planned a well balanced meal, as I had worked in the café as salad girl. We decided a black walnut cake would be nice. So we picked and shelled for more than an hour. I put plenty in so it would be nice and rich. We had an old wood stove. Guess what? The oven wasn't hot enough and the cake fell. I didn't figure I was whipped. I knew Dad loved cherry pie, so we opened up a can of cherries and pitted them as fast as we could and made pies. Again the oven wasn't hot enough. I demanded something to be done. So my husband went out and got a piece of rubber tire he had salvaged for such an occasion. In minutes the fire was roaring. A little later I looked into the oven, there was soot all over the pies. To my surprise, I went into the dining room, a cover off of an adjoining chimney cover had blew off and threw soot all over the table, in fact all over the room.

Tears were the essence then. We only had minutes left to hide the sooty table decorations, turn the table cloth over and sweep the room.

But dear old Dad bragged on the fried chicken and the pan gravy. Mom loved the salad and we scraped the soot off of the pie, covered it with ice cream and ate that.

The moral to my story, don't plan on a perfect show off dinner. I love to tell it to young brides that think adults never faced uncertainty.

FEBRUARY FOR 1998

To Whom It May Concern: Alice Laura Hartley

I love to write and scribble my thoughts.
I give my Father, Frank O. Henrikson, for many things he taught.
Honesty was first on the list!
Speaking of Dogs, in the manger, He never missed.
I needed the lesson and took it to heart.
I know what he told me was a start.
Maybe I didn't want to share---
He ask all I want is to be fair.
My disability, I didn't blame God.
I thought I was special, Gave life a nod!
I fit in the family with pride, I must say.
Didn't want to be a burden with care.
So I lend a hand with love to spare.
I love to garden and watch food grow.
I gathered and canned, shared goodness knows.
I accompanied my Father with music galore.
With love for music, it was shared more and more.
Thousand's of students played to my command.
I still thought God praised my helping hand.
God is love, with compassion for all.
We must thank Him again and again.
Feel "Special" He let us win.
P.S. We are, our own reflection.

Frank O.C. Henrikson's
Band
This was taken around 1906 or 1907.
at.
Rockville Nebraska, Papa is in
the center with a Trombone.-
written by Alice Hartley 1993

1904

January 14, 1904, a little blond baby girl was born to Frank O.C. Henrikson and Ida Mary Gray Henrikson's home in Rockville, Nebraska. To greet her were her sisters Jennie, Orah, and Mae. They named her, Eda Blanche Henrikson. Eda was born in a sod house at Rockville, Nebraska. She had a short time to be a baby. Her brother, Earl Carlene Henrikson came along. September 29, 1905. They were wonderful pals, were together constantly. Eda cut Earl's hair and threw the cuttings under the bed. I heard Mamma didn't really care for the style. When they sampled the chewing tobacco---again the evidence of two little teeth marks on the plug and Oh, so sick told the tale.

Papa had rented the place at Loop City, a few miles out of town. The landlord decided to paint the barn. He brought his son, Charlie. At noon time, Charlie, Eda and Earl decided to finish the paint job. I was too little and not enough experience to help. Oh, the trauma, was hard to endure. Oh yes, I showed June 15, 1907. A baby brother, Lloyd, in 1909. He passed away as a baby. Do you think I'm a tattle tale?

They said; June 15, 1907, My Mother gave birth to Alice Laura Henrikson. She said that was the last but two years later she was blessed with another son. The little fellow couldn't make it, In nine months God, decided to take him.

Our Father grew lots of food on our Nebraska farm. With all the severe storms we escaped harm. 1915 our Mother was called away. It grips our hearts with sorrow even today. 1919 we sold everything possible. Our homestead in Canada, it was different, I must say. The roots on the roads were shakers, but the freedom and friendships were greater. The lake was beauty, the fish were plenty. Mae and Eda were married by 1920. Dad and I, we battled the homestead together. I washed on the board, learned to cook, rode to school on a horse, no matter what the weather. I went to Calgary when I was 16. Came back to the U.S.A. when I was 18. Played music where ever I went. Worked in eating places, worked hard you can bet. 1928, to California we 3 couples went.

Depression was raging like a storm well spent. The boys worked in the fresh fish factory. Oh, what a smell! They weren't allowed in the house till they took off their shoes and changed their clothes and waited awhile. Gwen and I worked in the canning of tuna. We were dressed in white with rubber gloves. When I order tuna, that's what I always think of. Lee and I finally made it back to Idaho, via Oregon and Washington. Boise was our stomping grounds. I went into the music business full fledged in 1935. Groups were all I was allowed to teach for the government. Then I started on my own. I've had 35 years on the payroll for different organizations with music and dramatics. I've written hundreds of songs, plays and poems. Programs have been the highlight of my life, that I would write. I'm living alone now, I have a cute home, lovely studio. I'm making and playing tapes to sell. I just lost my friend, Verl Potts. I miss him so much. God Bless him where ever he is. March 1993.

88 YEARS 1995

When June 15, 1995 arrives, if God willing, I'll be 88 years old. It's amusing to meet different ages. The young are sometimes told about elderly people or senile. They wonder what do we remember, can we cope with modern times? When I was young and visited an eighty year old person, I told them good-by---Thinking it was over soon and I may not get to see them again. But you can be much older coping with every day. Still writing books, poetry, sewing, building, gardening, even pleasant to talk with. We want to be wanted and needed. We can call shut-ins, to cheer them, cook a special meal now and then. We can't swing family dinners any more, make a cake or a pie. I love to watch style shows and study them in the magazines. Then I think, Oh my, I dressed as a flapper when I was a teenager, floppy hats, short skirts made on the bias. They flipped when we walked and showed our garters. Yes, we've all gone through a teenage stage. When we've mastered that, we thought we had it made. Little did we know.

THE MISS PIGGY AT THE FAIR

Miss Piggy went to the fair,
To win a blue ribbon to match her hair.`
Celebrities were there you wouldn't believe.
They were there to gain the things to achieve.
Donald Duck was down on his luck,
He'd gone lame and lost his fame.
Rin Tin Tin was lookin' good, but wondered why
Lassie's friendship was misunderstood.
It came time for the AWARDS, and guess what?
There was the cow that jumped over the moon,
There was all the folks from the Looney Tunes "
Miss Piggy didn't plan to take a back seat,
So she sat by Kermy so sedate and neat.
Then the Judge said and "I quote"
You've got to be just mellow and sweet.
You've got to be nice, You've got to be neat,
Don't lie, Don't cheat, Don't blame your folk's;
And it's not the time to crack dirty jokes.
Now Morning is the time for chores;
Lunch time is the time to dine,
And don't gulp and eat like a greedy swine.
At night then you know that it's time for Prayers---
If you don't win try harder in the coming years.
Who deserves the "PRIZE", not a single
 soul bothered to rise.
Miss Piggy smacked the judge, and went
 home to eat her SUGARERY" fudge.

MR. AND MRS. SUGAR FOOT

Mr. and Mrs. Sugarfoot
Curious is the plan.
Find out what they're about.
Never can learn their route.
Out of sight, not out of mind.
Surely they're only one of a kind.
Eating Sweets is their plan.
Find out their Secret if you can.
Mr. and Mrs. Sugar Foot
Mystery is their Root.
If they got in the News
It would be the Sugar Foot Blues.

HUNGRY

Hungry to hear
You are dear to me.
You are sure to please,
The silver in your hair
Turned white.
Yes, white at night, alright,
Holding hands with delight.
No one to turn to,
No one to care.
I'm still hungry for someone to share
Lover's Lane, like littered
Backyard debris.
I can't complain.
My heart aches the same.
Lonesome Heart aches to blame
Empty Nest Blues

HEAVENLY FATHER

I speak privately to you,
You are loving and fair.
Who am I to compare?
I praise you, from time to time.
Please have faith in me.
I take your faith for granted.
I scan our planet,
Something to praise
In every corner of the Earth.
Four seasons to their worth,
Make your Home Sweet Home!
Or a home to be alone.
There's a light to light our way.
Please Heavenly Father
Light our Way.

MOTHERS DAY

If I had a Mother to call my own,
I'd write and say, Hello.
With all my Love, so you will know
I miss you so.

EASTER PRAYER'S AND EASTER BUNNIES

Fill our Hearts with plenty of
Money, Love, and Honey.
Little baskets found on the walk.
Susie; Basket matched her dress.
Easter colors are a Heavenly Bless.
Brother Tom found a nest,
The basket matched his vest.
Grand Mama always knows Best!
Bring it in and share what is left.
Share a Prayer is Fair,
Happy Easter Prayer.

THE MERRIMENT OF LOVE I SPEAK

Brings smiles and smiles
And Love beguiled.
The Shadows in the meadows,
Bring comfort to the ,Who knows?
Kind words are treasures
For the merriment of Love's Pleasures.
Every Heart felt song comes along
Lingers in our Heart
Makes us strong.
Love is just around the corner,
Never fear it's bound to loiter.
Two heart's beating in two quarter
Rhythms sake.
Merriment of Music is
Love Every time it Takes.

A PAIR OF FLAMINGOES

A pair of flamingoes found a home
That meant they couldn't choose to roam.
I put them in a shelter for the winter-
Named them Franz and Wittie.
To leave them out to shiver would be a pity.
True story.

THE OLD SHACK CAME TUMBLIN DOWN

The old shack come tumbling down,
Memories and all.
Even the clothes line,
Lest things lying round
My old Fishin Hat,
Bent an' faded
A few fish hooks
Stuck in the crown.
I've hoarded tall fish stories.
True as any fish story I knew.
Friend wrote the best,
I made up the rest.
California couldn't always
Tell the trout, gave it to me.
I eat it without a doubt.
This is true, they soon found out.

THE DOOR OF THE FUTURE

School has come to an end at last.
Yes, I would rather take a special class,
But it's time to fare for myself, what a task.
Open the door of the future.
I often dream of the fortunes and wealth.
There must be a way, who could I ask to say?
Uncle Jud has found it and lost it, he doesn't
know.
There's dad's brother stumbled into luck
called Happy Joe.
I must face the facts; How can I get on track?
Do I go with my peers? And live on the land?
Go with the crowd and dress dowdy de dow?
No, I'm ready to face the world, grow up,
Challenge my future, make it an exciting cup.
I'll seek a way of life, that fits my stride.
I know it's waiting for me, I won't let it hide.
I will stop, look and listen.
Think twice and accept advice.
Willing to learn. August 27, 1996.

FAMILY GET TOGETHER

The morning fresh, the dew is best.
They're drinking the best of the day.
Let us plan a boat ride,
Take the dog for a joy ride.
Hook a fish on a lonely hook.
Lucky Lou could catch one too.
A fish fry tonight, music playing,
Moonlight just right.
Shadows on the moon, love tune too.
Don't get excited, Mama's comin' too.
Dad will be there with us.
Melody of spoons, Oh, what a tune.

HELLO MY BABY, HELLO

Keeping me company,
Keeping me company.
Hello my baby, hello.
Let us take the boat
To the unpredictable Lake.
When the breeze turns to
The unpredictable wind.
I'll hold you tight
With all my might.
We'll cuddle every thing,
Everything, Pray is right.
We'll go back home tonight.
Keeping me company,
Keeping me company.
Good night my Baby good night.
Every things turning out right.

BIRTHDAY WISHES

If I could send this card by speed of light,
I'd have it there tonight.
I'd be with it to sample the cake.
Wish you good health, with no mistake.
May your day be special, I send my love too.
Sent to Muriel Campbell by Aunt Alice.

MISS UGLY

I painted a face
On a towel doll.
Yes, Miss Ugly.
New paints clabbered.
Like buttermilk.
George said;" She had
A dirty face."
Sue Carrol knew I
Tried to make a FACE!
I will cover her
Head with Satin,
Then paint it.
Even make it,
I crocheted it!

WILD ROSES

Wild roses blooming in the meadows,
Meadow larks singing again,
Springtime Melodies.
Babbling Brooks Splashing,
So the birds bathe on the wing,
It must be Spring.
May, day lilies nodding their heads
Mother's Day a few days away.
A gift of Love to make her day!
A Special Mom to call your own, per say.

LISTEN

Listen for the Wedding Bells,
Maybe they're Ringing for you.
Listen
Listen for the June Bug Parade.
Gathered to say,
Mr. Right is there and ready.
Listen
This is the day, You're goin' steady.
Take the bitter with the sweet.
This is your day, I repeat;
Listen
Leave the love to us.
June Love is so Sweet.
Listen

RUNAWAY BLUES

Good luck blues
Count your blessings
Wait for the news.
Someone is counting on
Good luck blues.
You can choose your new shoes,
Get ready for company too,
Bake a yummy yum cake,
Candied apples to take,
Aunt Anna made the punch,
Have puffy crème sandwiches for lunch,
Invite the guests early,
Meet at the park,
Sun is shining, and music is great.
We will start early, don't be late.
Happy Birthday.

FANCY FEET

I repeat Fancy Feet,
Danced away the night's retreat.
Her costume shimmered in the night.
A moon light delight
Silk a delicate Delight.
A cymbal of fright,
The ghosts were out to claim the right.
Home time, Fancy Feet back on retreat!

WHAT'S NEW

What's new, I'll be 92.
When nineteen ninety nine came along
I'd been told life is not a song.
Gay eighties, we danced the cake walk.
The early nineties, we enjoyed the bear hug.
Hobble skirt was fun to make,
A real step was hard to take.
The twenties, the flapper tried their wings.
The thirties, slowed the music and checked our sins.
The forties, cut down on the booze.
With no money, how could you lose.
The next dilemmas, makeover clothes on the make.
Look for flour sacks, second hand cloth on the take.
True story.

A GENUINE SMILE

A genuine smile will win every time.
Take it to the game for a while.
The spoils of tomorrow written on the wall,
A brow beatin' party to express their call.
Be ready to shout "ohla."
"Pepped us up," I'd say.
We came in first on every play
Wear a smile for the day.
Be ready to say, "Hooray," for the day,
We won.

HARBOUR LOVE

Harbor love with all your might
You'll find that love will win if right.
Brings faith we can relate to,
Happiness we can ornate to.
Hate is waist
Love is power
Time is ticking to the magic hour.
Let us be ready to accept the magic hour.
Colors will blend
Lights will lend
Change the world to the magic hour.
Love is power for the magic hour.

WISHING YOU WELL

Sometimes I send a message,
Good thoughts thru mid-air
To have faith when they arrive,
You will feel energy every where.
I can't tell the reason why,
If there's sunshine on your window sill.
Birds sing sweeter, you can tell,
God's watching over you,
He's wishing you well.

A smile is the best yet,
To chase away the Bad Luck Blues.

FARM YARD

When the moon gave up
And the owl said, "Who-who,"
The embers dying down
No more sparkle to display.
I counted the tick-tocks on the shelf,
Waiting for chimes to earn its wealth.
Early dawn will come along,
Playing on the new mowed lawn.
Too early to say good morning,
Too late to say good-night,
Count your blessings
Things will end up right.

2000 AUTUMN ARRIVED

Roses still peeping in the window,
Saying, "Hello."
Sunflowers drooping their heads,
Soon time to go.
Jack Frost paid a visit, as one would know.
Pumpkin faces smiling, this is their time to glow.
Pretty or ugly, what do they know?
Pumpkin rates still high, when it comes to a pie.
They go to the party
Whipped cream is naughty.
Halloween costumes would never show
Go with the flow.

JUNE NIGHT AND YOU

Keep a song in your Heart,
Let a smile take a part.
Tell the world you are getting
    Back on track.
Think of a way to usually say
    Tomorrow will be a better day.
God's Garden grew greener,
The tomatoes grew sweeter.
The Roses are blooming,
June is looming.
I'm assuming Moonlight,
Is in tune with the Mooners.
A June night, Moonlight and you,
In tune with a June night and you!

AN ESTATE SALE

As I stood among the memories,
One would know the broken dreams were gone.
Some selected frames of family,
I noticed pictures discarded and left
fluttering on the lawn.
The treasure of yesterday were thrilling,
As new owners went their way.
An Estate sale is the end of years, heartaches,
Memories and tears.
A doll left with scuffed up nose and one arm gone,
There she lay.
Then I noticed a ceramic vase of a Golden Angel,
Holding a golden harp.
An energy came over me and a spirit spoke to my
heart.
So alone as in need of a home.
Now it stands on display, I'm never alone.
Ashes and ashes, dust to dust.
September 17, 1995.

SPRINGTIME BLUES

The squirrels are eating my garden,
Magpies sampling it too.
The apple tree loaded with blossoms,
Pests waiting there too.
In my strawberry patch,
I've painted red rocks.
To see what the birds may choose.
I still have faith,
That's the way it goes.

SWEETER THAN HONEY

Love can be sweeter than Honey.
Romance can enjoy the romantic Moon.
True Hearts racing to spend time to Spoon.
Let time tell you and remind you,
Love is here to stay.
Soul Mates find a way.
If God puts us together,
He'll find a way for us to Pray together.
Days turn to years and God will find a way,
For us to stay together.

FAMILY TRUST

Family trust is a must.
When you catch a smile meant to cheer your day.
Tuck it in a corner of you heart to stay.
Different ones will hurl you off key,
Things to test your faith,
Maybe comfort to believe, some Faith to replace.
A re-kindled Love comes from above.
To build back Faith and Love.
Family Trust we are in need of.
Get on Line and turn time.
Family Trust is a Must.

A MEMORY OF LOVE

A memory lives in my heart.
We gathered our Dreams,
In Life's recollected scenes,
And we promise to never
    Let Life trample
True Love in its scheme.
We recited aloud our vows,
Togetherness made us proud.
A Prayer a Day,
Keeps harm away.
Don't let Life's other side.
Lead you astray,
Let Love lead the way.
A Memory of Love to stay!

THE GARDEN SCARE CROW

There stands a scare crow ---
Frosty and waiting for the shining morning sun.
To say "Hello" to veggies.
They need a welcome shower.
After the day begins,
The slugs use the beds of day and continue to
Chew their way thru.
The scare crow is showing age and wear,
You might find the scare is you.
P.S. second thought, could be me.
February 1999.

JUMP START

He gave my Heart a jump start!
I let on I wasn't true.
A playboy plays games.
With their Hearts, it's not new.
My hearts been broken,
I'm mending it back.
I don't plan on holding the sack!
Yes He's cute and calls me Honey
I Love to see him.
See me Monday, Tuesday,
Wednesday, Thursday, Friday Busy.
My Heart's ticking to lively Music.
The old tick tock keeps on moving,
I find it soothing.

I SAT OUT TO WIN

I sat out to win—
Looked for a place to begin.
I knew a Spirit at my side.
Knew I would live to abide.
Carry an upbeat light.
Extent, you're truly right.
Sprinkle a Sparkle on Sunshine.
Clear the mystery of limelight.
Strengthen the Friendship with Love.
Caring is close to need, in-deed.
Renew a friendship in need,
Send a kind thought,
By Spirit of Light.
Say a prayer to put things right.

A SWINGING DOOR

A swinging door swings both ways.
Sunshine is on the outside.
In gloom you will abide.
Pray to walk in clover.
Four leafs grow all over.
Tell the Irish story,
Good luck in all its glory.
Wear a shamrock in your shoe.
Green shoe laces will see you through.

BLUE MEMORIES

Memories so Blue,
Spent with you.
So Dear to my Heart.
I wish, if you knew,
Just to say good bye.
Was more than I could do.
Let's gather up our troubles
In an old back pack.
Settle up differences ---
Get on Track.
Let the Blue Memories
Be the Back Burner Blues!!

A BIRTHDAY

Another Birthday!
Should be with a Cheer.
I'll be Ninety Four.
Be thankful, Yes;
Wait and see.
Joyful I try to be.
I still play and sing
And write the things.
All my Family is gone.
Still Nieces and Nephews, Thank God,
To carry on
They think I'm a joker, when I carry on.
The Gray Family has always been caring
A Happy Life to carry on.
Smile and the world smiles with you.
Cry and God listens and hears me too.
When I cry.
To carry on

THE LEADER

Leading the way, not always kids play.
A storm came up to change our plans.
We served the lunch in cake pans.
The wind blew our paper cups away.
We sent for tin cups, saved from Mom's day.
We headed for the hall, rented for the day.
We spilled the platter of deviled eggs.
We ended up frying hot cakes to save the day.
Thanks Dee, you made the day! True story

WHO IS MISS DOT COM?

Miss Dot Com
Checks into everything!
She tells about the weather,
Rain or shine, or just fog.
Plays the stock markets bogs.
Surely can't tell about the task.
She has a comment on the cracks,
Even got a crack about that.
I've never met her,
Not doing so I'm better.
Miss Dot. Com travels to see,
She boggles my mind.
Keeps me company at times,
Check this out and see what you find!

I WEAR HIS RING

When I found someone to care.
Times were tough and worse for wear.
We took our vows
No Guests there to bow.
When we decided to begin,
I wore his ring.
Time got better in the Spring.
Our home we built was something!
Years stacked up, time went on.
I wore his ring.
Songs came on, music paid as we went along.
His way was paid, He couldn't stay.
Memories linger yet today.
It's lonesome I must say.
Still one thing, I wear his Ring!

FRIENDS

Friends don't just happen, we earn them.
They search for trust, dependable is a must.
A promise is adjustable, an excuse is
understandable.
A habit is understandable, too often leads
uncontrollable.
Don't let a promise be a figure of speech.
It will be a parable to meet.
Make your plans and meet it!
Thank God you don't need it,
Thank God you succeed.

Alice Laura Hartley

LIVING ON THE EDGE

Living on the edge,
Drinking up the sunshine.
Thankful for the happiness that seeps through.
After ninety years, days could turn to tears.
My Kitty cries, I can't hear her.
She's gone away, maybe to come back another day.
I love to live, live to love.
Come back, I need a Kitty to love!

MR. WHO

I met Mr. Who, guess what?
He seemed he was True Blue.
His shoes shined like new.
He played a tune on the rug.
But he didn't ask for a hug.
I wrote him off just a smug.
He played his tunes on a juice harp.
I thought it was smart.
Sounded nice to hear at the Park.
Don't kiss me---Stay Free.
The Bees are having their jubilee.
They Love my Honey Combs squeegee,
Keep lookin' there will be another, Mr. Who!

THE SECRET OF LOVE

The secret of Love is
Return it.
Kindness is the secret
Repose it.
Tune of Love endless.
Love grows with time,
Like a precious Chime.
Reproduced Children,
Moms and Grandparents,
Come along to Build 'em.
Mother and Fathers,
To play their part, Raise 'em.
Now I lay me down to Pray,
Guide us all the way,
Bless and Save them,
Aunts and Uncles!

SPRING 2000

The promise of Spring, looking for sunshine.
To welcome the flowers it brings.
Birds are on wing, mating again,
Making their nests.
Here again Robin Red Breasts.
Joy of spring, work to employ.
Meadow Larks toiling till dark.
Honey Bees buzzin' in the trees,
Working hard to achieve.
Brooks babbling in every nook.
Even the Hoot Owl took a look.
Springtime, a fresh time to listen,
For a Chime of Springtime!

SPRING AWAKENING

The flutter of a wing,
A reality could bring.
Disappearing berries real ripe.
Signs are a return of Spring.

The mellowing of the wind,
The lessons of the chilly Spring.
Natures time to awaken the blossoms.
The beauty of Spring is assume.

The faith of nature renewed.
The pussy willows are viewed.
The brooks and the valleys come to life.
The birds are in a hurry building family prides.

Baby birds cuddle and coo, twitter and cry.
When will Mom and Pop bird come by?
Sure enough they keep watch.
They keep time by Natures Clock.

TOMORROW

I plan to do better tomorrow.
I can't find the time today.
I wish I had said; "I loved you."
I found out tomorrow was too late.

FANCY RHYTHM

Rhythm in the morning,
Rhythm at night.
Fancy feet rhythm all right.
Dance to the tune of you guess who!
Turn your feet to, fancy feet rhythm.
You'll lift the spirit, to catch on rhythm.
First you bow, then turn and how!
It's God given fancy rhythm.

A PLEASANT LOOK

A pleasant look, a smile adorns the face.
A day to dry your tears, let a pleasant look take its place.
A smirk turns to a giggle, and leaves a smirk to take place.
It is time to check the weather, play a part to better.
Sentimental tells a time to care, stay on time on line.
Don't let smiles turn to giggles.
Smile a while, don't let it turn to riddles.

IDAHO

A capitol "I" for Idaho!
It carries prestige ten fold.
The "City of Trees" is proud to conceive.
Shade enfolds comfort, when in need..
Our mountains stand so staunch,
To protect the animals from babyhood to maturity.
Game is food to a table, a delicacy.
A way of life for every color and creed.
Mountain streams, babble and bubble in brooks.
Pan fry for cozy nooks.
Delectable delight to claim our own.
A capitol "I" for Idaho!

HUM A SONG

If I hum a song as I go along,
If I sing the lyric, I'm in savory.
Put the sunshine in your heart. I take it's not a maybe.
Hum, Sing, mixed with Love, it's a savory.
Let the sunshine in your heart.
Send a message of Love, as I mingle along.
Something is great, where right belongs!

HEARTACHES

Heartaches and death takes our loved ones.
It brings memories double fold.
Dearness and memories we hold.
We pray for comfort not bold.
We reminisce the joy to hold.
Gwen's church, her love home grown.
Work and music were forever known.
The others welcome her with pride.
Work to be done on the other side.

MAYTIME IS SPRINGTIME

Roses are showing beauty of love.
Lilac's perfume is to think of.
Gods promise of everlasting life.
Potatoes are sprouting for to grow.
Radishes are popping up to be just so.
Mary makes a sandwich and I glow.
Apples are undecided about the frost.
Onions make it, Frost or no frost.
Pray for peaches to be.
Cherries are starting to seed.
Idaho's garden is all we need.
Praise the Lord!

HOME COMING

Years have slipped by without an unusual sigh.
Time to get together, find out when and why.
I've always been the Mother type,
So I must plan the food that's right.
I'll make a stew and enquire what to do.
I'll start with a kettle of water, will do.
The one thing they know, I don't eat pork.
There's my oldest brother, doesn't eat meat.
I know little sister, veggies for a treat.
Sea food doesn't agree with Uncle Pete.
Mushroom is still a scare, to say the least.
When Betty died eating a mushroom feast.
There's Debby, reminded me no beans.
There's my friend, ulcers specify no greens.
I finely gave it up, bring a sack lunch.
When we all got together,
Hugs and kisses and enjoyed it very much.

AN ODE TO MY LIFE

If you want it---dream it.
At the age of two---just be it.
At the age of five---I sang it.
At the age of ten---I made it.
At the age of fifteen---I seek it.
At the age of twenty one---I married it.
Art and music played a part.
It answered to my dreams.
Rhythm keeps a ticking heart.
If you want it--- dream it.
I write music and play it.
Sing the lyrics, I mean it.
This old world helps you be it.
Just to be what you want, before you leave it!

FREE AS A SAND BAR

We are as free as a sand bar,
To stand where we may.
The waves slap the beach from day to day.
The frogs speak a noise,
Set on tuffets with poise.
Once in a blue moon it comes up.
There must be something to see.
The moon light shadows to be.
There came bathing beauties indeed!
A breeze brought music just their speed.
The frogs croak a rhythm you wouldn't believe.
The moon is a magic balloon.
There is magic, believe it or not!
Why, we almost forgot why we were there!

VALENTINE MEMORIES

When you look into an old box,
Where a collection of valentines stay.
Some said; "I love you, sure as morning dew."
Would you be my valentine if you knew?
I'll carry your books, if you let me look.
There are answers in the back of the book.
I have five pennies, I'll give you two, three for me.
I'll share a piece of mama's pie, or a taste of a
sandwich on rye.
I'll carry your books for a look into your book.
See you around, guess who XXX.

AN ARTISTS DREAM

When an artist takes a brush in hand,
one must have their thoughts in command.
Should it be a sea scape,
or a desert to explore and gape?
You select the season that maybe,
let it be springtime to surely please.
Now the time of day comes into play,
where is the sun,
that magic ray.
Maybe the sunrise will be up in due time, with pride.
Maybe the sunset will show long shadow strides.
We will just start with clouds,
clouds that will settle ones doubts.
Mountains in the distance scared about rocks and
crevices.
Caves are cold and creepy, that people talk about.
Let's get back to the desert with springtime magic.
Where silver on the sage glimmer and wave,
the thistles are blooming.
That matches the purple sage,
when pioneers traveled the dusty trails.
Sun flower seeds still prevail to mark their way,
what a thoughtful deed.
I'm going to start the picture,
I'm going to call my mistakes, happy little
accidents.
Like our artist Bob Ross, tells us we will make.

GOD'S GARDEN

God plants the seeds, then nature takes it's course.
To study the life of a tree, if it could talk, it would
say,
"Look what injured me."
I fought the big old trees that towered over me.
The sunshine was scarce, I was quite old before
The sun could even see me.
I knew I was meant to be important.
Then a lumber jack sawed down a tree.
Oh, how much better I could be.
I started to grow, 'twas so nice to know,
Some day I can be a part of a home,
A piece of furniture, maybe help to support a bridge.
What a joy to know I wasn't put here to be
trampled
From weakness, unkempt debris and smothered
In old rotted trees.
The way of life has many paths.

GLADSTONE

If I could travel at the speed of light,
I'd send good thoughts to Gladstone tonight.
I presume to find a right tone.
I found a new friend in Gladstone.
I find it's time to lend a hand.
When I write, just be a friend
I send a verse from time to time.
Think it over and make it rhyme.
To express, it should be said,
Keep sunshine and good thoughts handy at times.
We need praise and encouragement in many
ways.
Bring to mind the good old days!

LOVE SHOULD RULE THE WORLD

Love should rule the world.
A star from heaven is furled.
Let us be his helper.
Furled from heaven above.
Give the rain drops credit of refreshing love.
Violets peek up to be refreshed,
With springtime retreat.
Pussy willows nod their heads to say good
morning too.
Springtime in all its glory,
Ever lasting Life!

NINETY SECOND BIRTHDAY

As I reminisce of ninety two,
in my wildest I couldn't dream it.
We walked to school and church.
We were popular, I'll admit.
Played plays we wrote, sang songs, loved life.
Mother laid to rest 1915.
God needed her on his right.
Papa raised five daughters and a son.
His hair turned silver early,
To live longer as I read.
A zest for living's a need.
I didn't raise a family,
Borrowed my nieces and nephews,
Loved and cared for them, every one I knew.
June 15, 1999

THE BEAUTY OF PLANET EARTH

Shadows that fall on your plans,
Listen to your heart.
It could teach you truth.
The old tick tock is tired of its duties.
Let the sunshine come into your heart.
See beauty in the soil, it brings us little plants,
To adorn the window sill.
Not long for thrills, the heart, love and joy.
Sharing blossoms to loved ones you employ.
The beauty of planet earth.

PERHAPS

I can find a way,
To find a heart felt friend.
Perhaps---A friend to say good morning.
Send a good luck wish too.
I have an arm chair,
Exercise to be close.
With energy to build,
Builds a new you.
Heart and soul goes with you
Where ever you go.
A prayer, a song in your heart,
Good luck too.

AUTUMN ARRIVAL

Autumn arrived with a little nip.
Jack Frost blew a kiss and almost missed,
But he's standing by, Oh, so close.
He'll paint more pictures the next time he's here.
Where did the playful summer go?
We love the change of seasons, even tho.
Some flowers feel it's time to sleep,
And save their beauty for spring retreat.
Seeds that scatter and make their way,
To a new place and better space.
Trees drop their leaves to repair the soil.
To give trees vigor and strength to grow tall.
We are so at nature's command.
We wear the attire to fit each land.
We plan on the stars to guide our way.
We are so thankful the sun is here to stay.
September 1995.

VICKIE'S BIRTHDAY

V—Stands for Pep and Vim
I – Interesting Company
C—Calm Decision
K—Kind Out Look
I—Embitterment to Neighborhood
E—Every Commodity for Home Making

Vickie you give a bit of Love,
To each and everyone.
Of what we are so badly in need,
In your way of Life, you succeed.

WE WILL STAY TOGETHER

We will stay together forever and a day.
We will build our future, solve miffs, come as may.
Build a safety garden for children to play.
Swing and dream our troubles away.
Sunday breakfast, a delight to display.
Off to Church to meet people that pray.
Listen to their problems, we answered with dismay.
God willing, we will believe per-say.
Stay together forever and a day.
March 29, 1998.

HEAVEN'S WINDOW SILL

I heard it at my window sill
When the flutter of the breeze stood still.
An injured bird with a tale to tell,
Lay helpless from a gun shot shell.
It seemed so empty for it to be allowed,
Someone's senseless pleasure is what it's about.
The bird had a mission, each morning he came.
He fluffed his feathers and dusted the same.
So proud to cheer me, a morning delight.
He often whistled to his mate close by.
He gathered food for his babies in wait.
It was his duty, without a mistake.
I marveled his freedom to come and go.
His visit to me as a shut-in, could he know,
Only God, could know.
But maybe, he will know, maybe he will sing on.
Maybe on Heaven's Window Sill. July 28, 1995

GATHER UP YOUR MEMORIES

Gather up your memories,
decide the ones to keep.
Let the heart breakers rest awhile,
To forget them would be neat.

A pleasant memory, have for a keeper.
To think of the times with Mother,
We took a trip to Idaho to meet the folks.
Her time so short in this world, I shudder.

Families grow apart, change their names,
And to think back, lose track.
The family reunions are so precious,
Don't let your family come to that.

When we get old and feeble, yes.
If they call on the phone, are we able?
To say, I'm still here, not very stable.
If we keep our faith, we will meet later.
Will Heaven await us?
September 7, 1998.

1999 GO GO GO

It's time to pour the wine, nineteen ninety's on it's way.
Let's put our troubles aside,
meet it with a good time day.
Dust off the Golden Slippers Grandma left behind.
Let Grandpa play the fiddle,
all join in for a good time.
Join hands, dance up a storm.
Have a good time, there's no harm.
We can spruce up planet Earth.
Thank your lucky stars, for what it's worth.
Let T.L.C. rule Mother Earth.
We are waiting for a new beginning.
The millennium is waiting in the wings.
The stars will continue to shine.
The old romantic moon will show in time.
If the sun shines in our hearts.
Let the unconditional love take a part.

POP CORN RHYTHM

A pop corn treat was neat!
And the Birthday Fiddlers music was complete.
The pop corn barrel sat at my feet.
I clipped out the rhythm.
My niece brought me the spoons.
They pepped up the band.
The violins sounded grand!
The dancing has begun.
Sue Carrol and George danced and called it fun.
They were joined by guests, young and old.
What a joy I must confess.
I'm the Auntie came from Boise.
Pop corn rhythm was peppy and choosey.
I played and sang the Fiddlers Lament.
It was for the host, George Ward.
Good Luck and Happy Birthday was sent!
Oh Joy!

This poem was written by Aunt Alice after she came to Burley, Idaho to celebrate George Ward's birthday. We had invited the Old Time Fiddlers for the entertainment. Aunt Alice had a can of popcorn by her feet and she kept rhythm with her hands on the popcorn can. Gayla, her Grand Niece, brought her some spoons so Aunt Alice could make music along with the fiddlers.

After the fiddlers had finished their music Aunt Alice asked them if they would like to hear her play.

They all said "Yes." I don't think they thought they would hear music like they heard from the little white haired Lady! Aunt Alice could really play the piano, along with any other instrument you could hand her!

A LULLABY MELODY

A lullaby melody for baby and me.
My heart beats double to comfort you and me.
Melodies drift from trees as breezes come thru.
Baby is nesting, soft feathers to prove,
Their love for you.
A cry for love sends food,
Just for you and me. [baby and me]
A lullaby melody for baby and me!

TURN ON THE SUNSHINE

Turn on the sunshine,
Button up the blues.
The clean up man,
Will be glad together [boo hoo]
He'll find the old bottles,
With obsolete labels.
Stored in old and worn out shoes.
New papers talkin' fuze,
Join, what have you got to lose?
New rugs, dust the pillows,
Throw out last years willows,
Shine the mirrors.
Shed a tear, who's missin'!
Make a vow, we are in the now.

DREAM LAND

I just got back from dream land.
I let my dreams expand.
The moon was shining down,
Leaving shadows all around.
A wolf howling for his mate.
She answers, I'll be late.
The stars twinkled from a far
Don't wonder where we are.
My dreams made to expand.
Magic is waiting in dream land!

HARMONIZING THE BLUES

All colors aren't meant to meet.
Find a color that's in retreat.
Sky blue blends with colors repeat.
Blue eyes fascinate at times.
Blond hair brings memories to mind.
Baby face is sung to be cute.
Midnight blue is a hue,
Shadows on the moon, too.
Owl howling to break thru.
Harmonizing the blues.
Look for things that are new.
A blue eyed Blond to carry on.
Think it over, it could be new,
Check your timing, could be changing for you.

GOD'S POWER

God's power has the strength we allow it to be.
The luscious fruit depends on you and me.
Comfort of a home stems back to our command.
The care we give the land.
We look for a message on a cup.
A friendship expresses love.
We smile to warm the heart,
It denotes dearness of.
Our everyday hurts will heal.
Back to sunshine we'll steal.
Gods helpers to reveal.

GOOD LUCK CHARM

I found your Daddy looking for you.
Joleen, you are precious
Your brother Joe Joe loves you too.
Joleen, stardom is in your cards.
Joe Joe, stardom is on his list---best list.
Go together, stardom can't miss.
Let your stardom sparkle with dew.
Joe Joe will bring good luck to you.
Listen to the birds flutter wings.
Hum their favorite songs they sing.
A good luck charm can do no harm!

STRIKE IT RICH WITH LOVE

Strike it rich, Somebody cares!
You find the way, so they say.
Look for the good luck charm.
Find the way to the farm barn.
Hens cacklin' and roosters crowin'.
Take the high road you've known.
Black berries will ripen.
Free for God given.
A pie would be nice.
Ron, John and Earl plan a game.
Straighten up the place.
Thank you for a new face.
Joy to take place!

LISTEN FOR THE HARMONY

Listen for the harmony, that touches my heart.
Listen for the harmony that keeps love birds apart.
Listen, Listen, Listen, There are love notes a listen'.
One to three, one for me.
One to three, wait and see.
Love notes flutter, waving in the trees.
Spring time love notes, flutter, flutter in the trees.
Listen for the harmony in the spring time breeze.
Listen, spring time breeze!

LAUGHTER

L---Will lift the spirit.
A---Always the way to go.
U---Look for love to know.
G---Grow with ideas to success.
H---Have happy endings.
T---To know the way to go.
E---Every little thought.
R---Reminds us so.

1.   Good thoughts brings.
2.   Happy endings.
3.   Ideas grow to success.
4.   Ways and means give a reason.
5.   Think positive.
6.   Make do, it will come to you.

I LIVE TO LEARN

I live to learn, learn to live.
Always plenty to give.
I drink milk, listen to Welk.
To stay on the beam,
Write poems, sometime lean.
Enjoy sunshine,
Shadows when the moon shines.
A mystery for human kind.
Seek friendship, never give up the ship.
Love boat can be late, it's worth the wait.
I'm waiting!

HOME SPUN

Popcorn balls, Snapple drink,
A birthday Party, home cozy warm,
It caused us to think.
Old time fiddlers gathered to play.
Old favorites made up the day.
Popcorn rhythm is for young and old.
Hand Grandma the spoons,
Have Grandpa double up for rhythm untold.
Let the Grandkids have fun, too!
Call it Home Spun!

HEART ACHES

Heart aches and Death takes our loved ones.
Death brings memories double fold
Dearness and memories we hold.
We Pray for comfort, not bold.
We reminisce the joy to hold.
Gwen's Church, Her love home grown.
Work and music was forever known.
The others welcome with pride.
Work to be done on the other side.

SMILE AWHILE

Lift up your head and smile awhile.
Friends notice your happy style.
Go for a walk, with your Happy Talk.
Take your dog down the path to smell and sniff
His favorite Lodge.
If over ripe fruit is wasting on the vine,
Just take time to spend a little time.
Head for Home to smell the breakfast.
An aroma is good enough without digestin'.

TRUCKER

I was trucking along, singing a song.
Thinking of my stay at home, Mom.
She will be waiting, for the rattle of the gate.
With a hot meal waiting, even if I'm late.
Rover listens, listens closer when Mom cooks chowder.
Rover is lonesome and we call in our family.
We all look for love, delicious food, and fun.
Made with Love Home Spun.

MEMORIES OF ALICE HARTLEY 2001

The mail just came, I must check it.
Utilities so high, they say turn the lights low,
The air down, to bed early, and there you go.
Set morning coffee, fix your midnight lunch.
Don't let radio get us, even if they think they know.
Candy tastes better, Oranges sweet are better.
Tell them so.
I was supposed to go to East coast with poetry,
Too weak alone to go.
Such famous people to meet.
Would like to say "I told you so."
Don't tell me I'm old, 94 years!

LETS GO OUT ON THE TOWN

See what's goin' round,
Do we wait for sundown?
Start early, watch the parade go 'round.
Sun sinking in the west.
Time to gather up the rest, phoned a friend, they said;
"Thought you were dead."
No, I'm just waitin' for a real.
Hungry to be fed.
I've new hats to wear, I made, I swear.
We go where half orders to repeat.
Keep our bodies nice and neat.
Oh, there goes the phone,
Yes, I'm home!

SATURDAY MORNING

Saturday morning Mary, will drop by.
Give the garden a drink.
It's nice to know she cares;
Counts the tomatoes and squash
As she goes by.
Time of year for pears,
Canned or fresh is best.
Root beer clears the throat.
I still sing a favorite note.
Suppose to take poetry,
To a contest in August 2001.
To weak to tackle it alone.
No place to stay like home.
Home Sweet Home!

THE BOISE BRIDGE
[between Depot and Capitol]

Stood many years stately and tall.
Popma music dedicated the bridge.
1930 orchestra with Alice Holloway Hartley,
and Frank Henrikson.
Father Violin and me at the pump organ.
My dress was a 50 year old dress borrowed from
My sister-in-law.
As we came over the bridge,
We played Old Black Joe!
Then we kicked up a square dance
Of course I had a bonnet on. [true story]

BEE'S WERE BUZZIN'

Bee's were buzzin' in an old apple tree.
None of Mom's apple pie for you or me.
Some bees were making honey nearby.
Grandpa knows how to rob the bees,
Don't tell mommy!
Any time to please, I think I'll put on his bonnet.
It looks so easy and neat, might as well have a
treat!
Grandpa had a secret, let him keep his old bonnet,
With all the bees on it. I'll just rob a honey comb.
Leave Grandpa's bonnet alone!
Gods power as we reap!

OLD FASHIONED CHRISTMAS

Make a list, check it twice.
Don't forget Grandma, cookies are nice.
Grandpa might tell you what not to do.
Buy him something he will cherish too.
There is Mom with shoes the dog chewed.
And Pa counting the money to get us thru…
All and all I count on Santa too.
Surely an Auntie will knit a cap and mittens too.
Our Uncles love candy too.
All and all Merry Christmas to your Family.
Happy New Year to see you through.

OUR LOVE WITHERED
ON THE VINE

When good time Harry spent time around.
He was so polite, He brushed his cat at night
Took her for a walk in the morning,
While the dew was fresh and the air was best.
I was Second Hand Rose!
Second choice, Heaven knows.
I hum songs, no longer cheers my heart.
Although shine of the sun can play a part in time.
Even though our love has withered on the vine.

A CHRISTMAS VISIT

Brings joy to my heart!
Petersons brought their Granddaughter for me to
see.
A dream I would not miss.
She kissed my doll, took the brown boy home.
I bet to a good home.
She liked my art work.
Wrote on her Christmas Cards.
Notes one couldn't believe.
It wasn't easy, I'd say hard.
She speaks with ease, with words to please.
She suits me to a tee.
Come back Matty to visit.
She visits with such ease.

DAY DREAMS

Day dreams last a life time.
I dreamt I was a Queen Bee.
Waiting for a Title.
My pony passed on, I still have a saddle.
I kept the bridle.
What about a side saddle?
I could bring in the cows,
When it was 5 o'clock now.
Ride in the meadow to tell.
Listen for the right bells.
Day Dreaming Hobby,
Seem to grow things to tell.
Answer the phone, Everything's well.

IRISH LUCK

Pray to walk in clover,
Four leafs grow all over.
Tell an Irish story,
Good luck in all its glory.
Wear a shamrock in your shoe.
Green shoe laces, will see you through

SHOW ON THE ROAD

Let's get the show on the road.
Take the old banjo off the wall.
Tune up the trap drum set for a ball.
The old Honer accordion, back on the job.
Bring back the old soft shoe.
Harmonize the voice work,
Kate and Alice turns will do.
Tenor guitar to soup up the rhythm.
Time to get on the road.
Requests to give 'um!

THE HISTORY OF THE SKIRT

In times gone by, the bustle skirt,
Was a favorite of ladies to work.
Ballroom dancing to the strains of Stroud,
Famous waltzing, they so much did love.
The hobble skirt came along, so short lived.
Couldn't become popular, it just wouldn't give.
In the twenties, the flappers came along.
Skirts made on the bias, they flipped
and showed the knees.
We were traveling fast, low waist band, even me.
In the forties music slowed down, so did we.
With the skirts at a decent length, trust me.
Then came the mini skirt, shocking to see.
I thought it was brave, suited some to a tea.
In my life the skirts have been several lengths.
I couldn't imagine but what a jinx,
Now they go skirtless, they think it's great.
Will before the turn of the century be too late?
April 30, 1998.

MY WATCH WON'T WIND

My watch keeps stopping, so I can't know the time.
It really doesn't matter, when you don't keep score.
I find worry is just a bore---
If you're wasting time, you don't want to know.
Sometimes you wonder if the days aren't slow.
Hunger can come and go, if you just eat shakes.
Maybe your tummy won't show.
When my friends call and say,
"What a nice day, what did you do?"
I sip my coffee and hum and haw, finely say,
"I haven't a clue."
Time keeps on going and that's the fact.
I just keep on working on this and that,
With new projects every day.
September 1995.

SEASON COMPLETE

Two Thousand showed up.
We still share the Stars and Moon yet
They are on duty, as usual.
Faith, Harmony, don't forget.
If spring is on it's way,
Get ready to display.
Little plants are waiting for their day.
To blossom, bloom and grow.
Represents their faith, you know.
Their timing is ornate.
If we had the faith of a mustard seed.
Settle down, and I repeat;
Plant the seeds; let springtime showers,
Feed the veggies and flowers.
Another season complete!

THE FISH STORY TALE

Did you ever hear this fish story tale?
A cat fish can wiggle and waggle,
And walk on his tail.
They can sting , you know, and have to be skinned.
Pan fried in butter, yummy, good to the end.

THE OLD LAZY "H" RANCH

Had a gate by the barn.
If the cows got out,
Old Shep sounded the alarm.
The calves close by, in a pen of their own.
Their Mamas knew they could atone.
Fed first to quench their thirst.
Harvest is on its way.
Corn cribs adorned the yard.
The dogs stay on guard.
Potatoes ready to dig.
Squash seasoning to a nig.
County Fair going on here and there.
Farmers delight with time to spare!

A WISH FOR YOU

May each snow flake,
Sparkle with a Christmas wish for you.
May each snow flake bring,
A joyous holiday back to you.
 There can be memories in every card.
A tinkle of love in every bell.
A heart felt story we can tell, again and again.
A Merry Christmas farewell, to when.

SUNSHINE IS A WIN

Read your poems again,
The sunshine is a win.
If you "Loose" a Love,
Not the last chance you have.
Always another left in the sea.
Don't pine over spilt milk, believe me.
Our Freedom is so "precious," See!
Enjoy looking, believe me.
Admit you are Lonely,
You are not the one and only.
Pretend you are happier than a honey bee.
People will seek you out to see.
Talk of old love's,
That kept your heart a breeze.
Lookin' for a new excitement,
Any time you please.
Who knows? Good Night.

BELIEVE IN YOURSELF

Believe in your self, your Dreams will come true.
Let the sunshine in your heart.
Call a friend to take a part.
You can be lonely, call the one and only.
Force bulbs to bloom early.
Easter Sunday, brighter than springtime,
Sweeter than Honey Candy.
Eat leftovers on Monday.
Believe in yourself, put your troubles on a shelf!

THINGS TO TRY

1. I tried pounding jello on the wall,
    Even glued it so it wouldn't fall.
2. Popped pop corn without a lid, I can't tell
    you all I did!
3. When I paint a winter scene, mess it up with
    Fiddlers green.
4. Get ready for the best you've heard. Say
    hello to a deaf bird.
5. I've tried eating milk with a fork. Sporty way.
6. I tried a juice harp with a 10 pieced band. Not
    for stay.
7. Cry me a river before it's gone.
8. At 94, look for a shoulder to cry on.
9. Lie about your age!
10. Ask for sympathy at this stage.

MELLOW MOUNTAIN MOON

We are dancing to the music of
Mellow Mountain Moon.
I'm holding you close, listening to the heart
beating,
In time and tune.
I'm in love with you.
Our dreams came true.
Stars twinkle down from above.
God's spirit sends love from above.
Violins blend in harmony.
Love Birds bill and coo in matrimony.
Let us dance 'till the break of day.
We'll be back, come as it may.
Mellow Mountain Moon, our Love is here to stay!

BOO HOO

You got me crying for you.
Why, I really never knew.
Rainbows dancing on your shoulder.
Sweetie pies by the hour getting bolder.
You never mention Wedding Bell Chimes.
When we're together, there could be times.
Boo Hook, if you knew, I want you for mine.
Size seven is my ring size.

SIDE BY SIDE

Side by side to harmonize.
A wish that could come true.
Talk about the weather and
Ready for True Blue.
Count the days and count the ways.
Christmas coming soon.
Lots of Christmas joy in every tune.
Jingle Bells keep ringing,
Morning night and noon.
Holidays light the way,
With an Old Romantic Moon.
I'm glad Mom and Dad used their
Romance to spoon.
I'm number 8 in time to get in line.
The last girl to get on the vine.
Lucky Me.

ALONE WITH A DREAM

Down a pathway star beam.
Loved ones gone, their dreams set free.
Could it be real for me?
Renew your dreams,
Down a pathway to believe.
Bless the sunshine from time to time.
Bless the perfume that fills the air at times.
We are blessed by our deeds.
Let our garden be free of weeds.
Be ready to share our needs!

2001 SHOULD BE FUN

It's been planned by everyone.
New ideas, sun of a gun.
Say what you please.
Money doesn't grow on trees.
Seniors headed for make-do.
Remodel the old wardrobe.
Salvage the new.
Leather shoes will see you through.
Shoe shops waiting, new heels too.
Turkey Roasters will do.
Safer then, than now, even new.

AT THE AGE OF 94

Looking back at the youth of today.
We were called Flapper Queens.
Looking back, nothing to say.
We had worn every length of skirt made.
Hobble skirts went away soon.
You had trouble with stepping too soon.
Horse back riding, a laughable boon.
We dropped the waist lines,
Split the skirts
Shortened the skirts and painted our knees.
Flipped them as we walked,
And did as we pleased.
Danced cheek to cheek, tinted our legs.
Now nylons to buy.

HOW WILL I KNOW

How will I know?
Will there be Spring in the Air?
Will there be Baby Birds?
Will there be Mama bird coming by?
Fresh and new Birds Nests?
Pussy Willows waving in the breeze?
Spring is back, ever Lasting Life.
A promise of Lasting Life.
Baby Fish babbling in the brooks.
Just a look is all it took!

SANTAS SCOUT

Papa's scout talk 1916.
I met Santa's scout today.
He usually doesn't denote his purpose.
I check the families,
Do they relinquish gifts?
Conducts in the miss.
He found boys shooting Mama Birds.
They were taken off Santa's list, so I heard.
He didn't list the chores they had missed.
Papa said, "He asked me my list."
Answered "I haven't checked it yet."
You better be good to get the gifts you should.
I'm better than good, Santa Claus!

WALK IN THE SUNSHINE

As I walk in the sunshine,
I often compare the stars to the moon.
God, asks us to share.
If we took a notion.
We can't own the ocean.
We are not here to stay,
Visiting , I would say.
Flowers to enjoy, compare each day.
Veggies and food, each year, we pray.
May God, prepare us to find a way.
Let us go home when he prepares us a way.

RHYTHM AND RHYME

A musician can get by it every time.
They'll polish their clothes till they shine.
Put on an air, you will notice.
Brighter than thine.
Find a joyful way to say,
You look so nice today.
Take you out, when it wasn't planned.
Special care in their command.
Don't fall for a soap box air.
They use that game there and where.
Enjoy the day!

CHRISTMAS 1935

Mother made a batch of soap,
Darned Fathers sox.
The harvest of ice was stored in straw in a box.
Fourth of July, Ice Cream was sure to please.
Lemon aid, made in the shade.
Grandchildren had the lemons to squeeze.
Ball games, lots of fun.
Put the ball away when the band begun.
When the races started,
Bare foot was no disgrace.
Races over, then to the pond.
To refresh their feet, how neat, comfort beyond.
A down south Christmas 1935.

"WINGIN' IT"

It's tough without wings.
Our chosen people have waited years.
I dreamed of a rig too, that swings.
Up over the trees carried by the breeze.
Up among the birds.
Beautiful things I could see.
Am I "special" no just a will,
To help progress to proceed.
Pedals of an old fashion organ,
Bellows to build pressured air,
Can raise us up above the trees.
Enjoy the freedom of the breeze.

SOME DAYS

Some days I'm lonesome and blue!
Some days when the sun shines,
A dream so bright and new.
Sometimes I can't cry if I knew,
The world was falling in dew.
Force a bulb to bloom in June.
Play a Happy tune,
My Birthday is coming soon.
Send your cards out in due time.
Try not to be late with mine.
Keep on line is a good sign.

A HAPPY CHRISTMAS

Papa's Christmas sock,
Hung on the back of a chair.
Brother's bigger than mine.
They decided it would be fine.
Papa said "Alice, yours is too tiny".
So I hung his sock, finely.
Sure enough, Santa, put a tin headed doll in mine.
A Roly Poly for Brother, a happy time.
Early to bed, always said.
Waiting for Santa, a dread.
We smelt cookies baking,
After we were put to bed.
A Happy Christmas with Family,
And lots of goodies!

GOD BLESS AMERICA

Enjoy your day.
A new President on the way.
May he be the one to stay.
Too bad we can't all have our way.
Keep a safety lock on U.S. Business.
Pray for our Best Wisdom.
Years spent under Foreign Stars.
Red, White and Blue, Love for Uncle Sam.
Brought my Love back to you from a far.
A Home forever to stay.
God Bless America!

FLOWERS FOR EASTER DAY

I've been waiting for the door bell and listening.
Maybe it's someone I've been missing.
I've read the cards with faith and regards.
Things will have to happen at large.
Keep a wish in your heart.
That plays a big part.
Enjoy sunshine, flowers thrive and come alive.
Plant Spring Bulbs in an Autumn sunny window.
In the Spring, give them light and plant food.
Ready to bloom soon,
Easter is on it's way.
Flowers for Easter Day.

IF I HAD THE WINGS OF AN ANGEL

If I had the wings of an angel,
I'd travel by speed of light.
I'd mingle with flying doves delight,
And listen to learn doves.
Brides happiness, so bright.
Heavenly evening on it's route.
To touch a tender lip, no doubt.
Love songs linger thru the trees.
Make a promise in your heart to please.
A Heavenly Breeze!

HAPPY NEW YEAR

Christmas late cards,
Happy New Year-----
2001, We're so glad to be here.
Spared to be "Special".
Give us a chance to make a wish.
Happy New Year for sure!
I planned a Happy New Year,
To wish it would come true.
Let us say if we knew,
Let "Special" Days come true.
Clouds in the sky,
Let the wind blow them by.
Rain drops kiss the morning dew.
Fresh Sun Shine back, we welcome too.
For a nice day to enjoy too.
Wishing you the best 2001.
Let it be second to none.

YESTERDAYS EYES

We remember Beauty.
Songs we remember.
We reminisce the mountains in their glory.
Seasons that change,
Beauty to be hold a story
Sold of Natures Way from day to day.
Remember yesterdays eyes, are here to stay
Remember the beauty of yesterdays eyes, We pray.

EGILA
Lee
1999

ON LINE

I shined my shoes and got on line.
Everything is going fine.
We danced the Spin,
Decided what and when.
The Moon, light blues
We danced when we got the news,
Still every thing O.K.
Oh, by the way, lost our shoes.
Then we were up set.
Wondered what to do, you bet!
We took 'em off to cool our feet.
We can't find them, "I repeat"
Now we set in the shade.
Until we get it made.
Get off line, better luck next time.

2000 ARRIVED ON TIME

We are urged to get on line.
Enter net asking it to build.
Benefits promise to meet.
An unusual guide line,
Wait and study your rights.
Let time tell when alls well.
Let them live, and let live.
Wait, let them give and give.
Nothing gained, nothing lost.
Wait stand by them at no cost.

LET LIFE COME AS IT MAY

Better luck could be on it's way.
The fall hay is in its shelter.
Jam and jelly couldn't be better.
We stacked all the wood we could.
Took care of all the veggies we should.
The old Mother Hubbard Cupboard is full
Time to put up the Christmas lights
Spread Christmas Cheer!
Send Cards and Wish A Happy New Year,
For 2001!

NEW YEAR JOY

Dry your tears, a New Year.
Bury the hatches, it's close and near.
Look for your special star,
It twinkles where ever you are.
Make a wish, let it be your dream.
Build a thought to be a please.
Don't be an open book.
Write a book, stories where ever you look.
You can be "Special" because,
Happy stories to recall.
Sunday school for all.
The pond where frogs go along,
Pollywogs turned into frogs.
And the Fishin' in the pond.
We grow and learn, a life of concern.
Happy New Year!

DON'T ANSWER EVERY WHIM

Don't answer every whim.
Good luck can be slim.
Take a dog along the Green Belt.
Vote to your ability.
It's a gamble, you can bet.
Make up your mind.
Be pleased who ever wins.
They will be the best to begin.
Passed down for all, a lesson for all.

SUGAR FOOT

Sugar Foot lives in the mountain terrain.
Lonely and travels in places of friendly animals to train.
Stays to walk in sand, never leaves a track.
To keep his secret in command.
Goes south in the winter, follows the Birds of Paradise.
Feast on different unfortunate demise.
Sugar Foot, stories for the wise.
Let it be a mystery to prize.
Enjoy the woods, Be wise!

WEAR A SMILE IN YOUR HEART

Wear a smile in your heart.
You can always send a love dart.
Be prepared to take it back.
If it doesn't fit the act.
Sisterly love can take a part.
Live forever in ones heart.
Popular care, givers are God given.
Welcome to the other side.
Comb their hair, bring back the curls.
Let the gray show, A love
To prove white shows swirls.
There's proof of a place for
Grand Ma's and Pa's.
Keep the joy of Santa Claus in our hearts.

FOUR ANGELS FROM AFAR

Each claimed a star.
"God" given, "love" given.
L. Stands for love.
O. Overly helpful.
V. very concerned.
E. Evil backwards is live.
They stand so staunch and true.
Untouchable, as I knew.
A reminder of Heaven awaits.
Their power of Golden Gates.
Could they select the next to enter? Date?
Be the ones to comfort soul mates.

LIVE AND LEARN

Live and learn, learn and live.
Always count on Above
Dreams sent with Love, can come to you.
Sent with Spiritual thoughts.
To tell you, could be true.
Look for the signs.
Bless the sunshine,
Study the times---
Always yours and mine.
Look and you shall find.
Comfort, Happiness of the kind,
Home Sweet Home! It's been there all the time.
Cook with Love, send good vibes.
That's the reason for Reason and Rhythm.

HIGHER THAN A KITE

I'm higher than a kite,
Unpopular as an unpopped corn,
In a wind storm in a Nebraska snow storm.
It didn't last, it blew over into Wyoming,
In a Blizzard Blast.
Now the Sun Shines, Guess What?
I met Mr. Who!
Welcome, he just knew.
Together again, Will do.
We'll plan our Future,
For dreams to come true.
More Happiness than we ever knew.
Bless our Home.

MERRY CHRISTMAS

Sparkles of Diamond in the snow.
Christmas, where ever you go.
The tinkle of Bells, you might know.
Our Church lit to welcome its guests.
I peeked in the kitchen, it's the best.
Mamas cookies stood the test.
It's an Old Fashioned quest.
Members none to be alike.
Treated to Pray this Holy night.
Even Santa asked to stop by.
I've set the scene, it's on the beams.
Music, singing and gifts for all.
Good eats and welcome to all.
Merry Christmas and to all a good night.

KITTY CAT LOVE

Kitty cat love is what it's about.
Tom has been scouting, to find out what's on his route.
Kitty cat knows to share,
She loves her comfy chair.
Let Tom roam here and there.
I'm looking for Mr. Right.
I could get lucky tonight.
Tom Junior is on the prowl.
I've been lookin' for howl's.
Kitty cat love comes and goes.
There will be another goodness knows.
Time to take a bow.

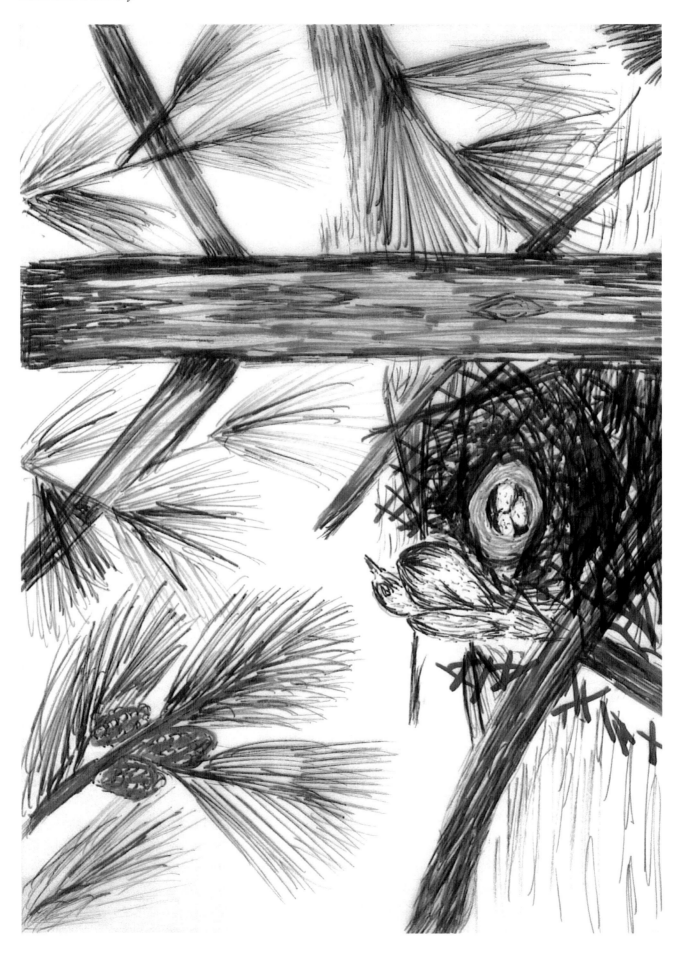

BLESSED

Blessed are the ones that care for their fold.
Blessed are the caring they have and hold.
Waiting and watching, trusted have and hold.
Blessed are the ones untold, sunshine follows.
The trusty souls brighten your pathway.
As it brightens our souls, our paths will brighten.
As our path unfolds, a tour watching young and old.
The pathway we follow, enriches our soul.
Amen, Praise Him!

CRY ME A RIVER

The summers gone---
Send the birds South,
Where they belong---
Snow birds stay and carry on.
They brighten the morn,
With twitter and song.
Halloween so special,
With costumes and treats to carry on.
We gather up the harvest.
Food so prolonged.
Thanksgiving never forgotten,
With celebrations and songs.
Oh Shucks, here comes Christmas.
Where we all come alive.
Forget the River,
We will all survive!

BRING BACK THE GOOD TIMES

Bring back the good times.
Dates were over by eight, Don't be late.
Bring back the good times.
We went to the park, to listen to the larks.
Bring back the good times.
Ice cream served on special days.
Good old times.
Bring back the good times.
We expected respect, we never grew up.
Root beer the top of the day.
Bring back the Good Time today.

DREAM ON

Dream on, I'm looking for Mr. Who?
Would his voice be mellow and true?
Soft and inviting for a lovely evening.
Tho' the moon's behind a cloud.
Love could be just so, tho'.
Even noise so loud, I awakened with a start.
It over taxed my heart.
Let Mr. Who be, you know "Who"
Dream on it can come true!

CHRISTMAS IN IDAHO

Listen to the Christmas Bells,
Sparkle in the snow.
Santa listen, Are you there?
In bed fast asleep.
There were secrets to keep.
Mom didn't ask for her ring.
Dad let on, his ears to warm with fur.
Let us go to Grandma's and Grandpa's,
Chop some wood.
Make sure the House is comfy warm.
Help feed the animals in the barn.
Listen to the Christmas Bells,
Sparkle in the snow.
Christmas in Idaho!

THE OLD MILL POND

The old mill pond iced and ready.
Get the briquettes ready.
I'll get the best hot dogs in town.
Last years list is okay.
Tonight at eight, be on their way.
Bring some records to play.
While we skate and play,
Invite Grandpa to change the music of today.
Pretty or loony, Who cares, if the moon is spooney.
The camp fire lights dancing with the shadows.
Hot dogs dancing in the kettles.
Time to serve the food, we deserve.
Hungry or not, eat up, it's all we got.

UNPREDICTABLE

I'm as unpredictable as a birdie shot.
Sure I'll take a go at it.
An undecided thought can change it.
The wind blows west and the Birdie goes East.
A disappointing Holiday feast.
Bring home the bacon, Grandma's eggs for the takin'.
Biscuits baked to a perfection from Mom's oven.
Take a day off from golfin',
Enjoy Grandma's cake from the oven.
Build up the wood pile.
Listen to young son's stories, they tell in style.

APPLE BUTTER

Hot apple butter and pumpkin pie.
Ron bragged about his hot apple butter.
Mom bragged about pumpkin pie and hot apple butter.
Ron's grandpa enjoyed hot apple butter,
And apple pie from the oven.
Grandma enjoyed her apple pie and apple butter
From the oven.
Drop in at the Peterson's for a Holiday Treat.
I repeat!

RON'S HOT APPLE BUTTER

Ron's hot apple butter and Mom's apple pie.
Invite the family, Don't let on why.
Keep stewing apples with honey and rice.
If they ask for a taste, serve them twice.
Mom can tell about the apples she had.
Ron can brag about his apple butter, was the fad.
Cooked in the oven, Grandma's favorite love.
Grandpa's favorite biscuits, out of the hot oven.

HOLY GHOST A COW

The phone broke down, what to do now.
The T.V. gave up the ghost, I missed T.V. most.
Loren showed up with T.V. and remote control.
How long can I use it? As long as you need it.
Loren, the Lord thanks you, and I do too.
And he loves you for your kindness.

AUTUMN LEAVES

Autumn leaves changing colors.
They will give up when weather's colder.
Apple harvest nearing, Idaho fruit preserving.
Old cook books, referred to for learning.
It's been said Grandma's apple butter,
Has been said "The best to be had".
Carmel apples was Mom's favorite.
Carmel apples, a favorite for Dad.

I'M BACK

I'm back, with all the love, I've always had.
Kisses in the morning dew.
Pleasure in the evening too.
Pleasure we often knew.
I'm back to prove my love for you.
I took a trip through rose colored glass.
I'm back, to ask my love back.
Dad learned so much while I was gone.
Mom, humming her favorite song.
I'm back, to tell the world, I'm back.

HELLO FROM IDAHO

A little bird stopped with a message,
"Hello from Idaho."
Resting on my window sill.
Holidays to revise a memory if you will.
Love and caring still.
Merry Christmas and happiness for the New Year.

LONESOME

Lonesome for a ride in the valley.
They tell me leaves are back.
Fresh and green.
Pussy willows waving in the breeze.
Mushrooms popping up, to be gathered free.
Fried in butter, for the eating.
Red robin stands staunch and true.
Waiting for her babies due.
As tho' she knew.
Lonesome for a ride outside in the valley.
Make my dream come true.

THE GOOD OLD DAYS

I'm lonesome for the good old days.
Even the huggin' and kisses.
For Mom's apple pie,
Baked in the old fashioned kitchen.
The children carried wood, to bake the goodies.
Prepared in the old fashioned kitchen.
Pop was always fixin', fixin' in the shop.
Finishing leather, getting ready for the kids shoes
he was fixin'.
We ate together, prayed together.
Still stay together.
We had good ways together.

FAMOUS QUOTABLE QUOTES
Compiled by Alice Hartley 2000

We can't recycle wasted time.
Then compare what lies within.
Don't follow a path, take a pathless trail.
A special path will prevail, I say.
Well done is better than well said.
You may delay, time will not, they say.
Evading today is no escape for tomorrow.
We are what we repeatedly do.
Excellence is an act.
We all wish we knew, to see us thru.
What ever you are, be a good one. Abraham
Lincoln

THE WONDERMENT OF LOVE

Is a good luck wish I'm thinking of.
Wish for a new moon, to show us a way.
Ask for a lucky day.
A new found friend could change the way.
Don't plan to go astray.
No change at all could be the way.
Home Sweet Home to stay.
Make later plans another day.
Christmas is on it's way .
Invite the home Folks,
Put on a Christmas Cheer.
Will last a happy memory for a whole year.

LUCKY LOU

Lucky Lou came to town,
Just to check what could be found.
He found people were out to run around.
Lucky Lou played tunes on hickory sticks.
The juice harps at the parties mixed.
The violins fiddled up a tune.
The down south voices you can hear were there
too.
We praised the Lord to ask for help.
Set the table with food of wealth.
And thanked the Lord for our Mama's help.
Hot biscuits and gravy and apple pan dowdy.

A MAGIC MOMENT

A magic moment spent with you.
I couldn't believe it could come true.
A magic moment seems so short.
I kissed him good-bye at the airport door.
A card sent to say "Hello".
Made my day, one would know.
We used to wait at the gate.
Now we wait by the phone,
Till we know it's late.
A magic moment, keep phoning.

A SINGING TEA KETTLE

A singing tea kettle and a covered butter dish.
Mom's, Moms favorite buttered honey.
Down on the Sunny Brook Farm.
Shep is waiting for the oven alarm.
We take some goodies to the boys in the barn.
The chickens didn't cackle,
The roosters didn't crow.
Don't bring us the subject,
It will soon, be soon enough, you know.
We lay eggs for Easter,
Bring them babies for Spring.
If that's not enough to-day,
We can't furnish everything, I say.

JANUARY 2000

Sugar up the blues, get on line;
Be on time, everything is news.
Even shine your shoes.
2000 is here so abide.
Rock and roll is old, shimmer and shake.
New, I've been told, you've got to be on line.
When the girls are bold, shimmer and shake.
They say what it takes, you don't have time to mold.
Go with the flow, I've been told.

HOLD ME WHILE I CRY

I'm denying you aren't mine.
If I could steal your heart away,
Could it be just child's play?
Sweet Hearts come and go.
 In my heart if I could know.
Our hearts beat in rhyme.
They could be God given.
Just hold me while I cry.
Even tho you are not mine,
And bring a sigh.
The rumble of the thunder,
That dances across the sky.
Tells us Heavenly Spirits,
Threaten our lives to abide.
If we could hold hands with loved ones.
Promise safety, second to none.
Let Love stay and faith play.

AN APPLE A DAY

An apple a day keeps the doctor away.
I picked a lemon, grew in the garden of love.
Where they say, only apples grew.
I found a thorn on lovers lane.
Where they say only love remains.
What to do? Find a new love.
A new promise to harmonize.
New rose buds and goodies,
Fun as you find it.
Painted till you admit it.
Let fun pay a visit to you.

IF I WERE A CHINA DOLL

If I were a china doll,
You could break my heart in a million pieces.
But I'm a raggedy ann doll,
Trying to make things stay in stitches.
I want to stay in my home.
I live alone, my husband passed away in eighty-five.
Again I had to atone.
The state took our home for a road.
The nineties have been a lonesome go.
I would like to find a way to keep my home,
And enjoy the rest of my days.
I'll be ninety four in June.
Home Sweet Home, a favorite atone.

A MOMENT TO DREAM

A moment to dream, as short as it seems.
Tick tock goes the heart beat.
As unusual as it seems.
A dream set a side, to enjoy as it beams.
Years has dimmed the whims that may have been.
Could it have been revised, just to be?
Brought back for me. Love is here to stay.
It has to be God's way.

THE JOY OF LIVING
For seniors in the sunset of life

I learned the joy of living, take the bitter with the sweet—
Start each day with expecting an adventure,
You might like to repeat---

Let blue Monday be the time to check on shut-in's---
Take time out to meditate, to neglect is a mistake---
You can dream of days gone past
Don't dwell on what if and what was---
What you worry about never comes to pass---

If you're lonely make a friendly phone call---
To relax, a refreshing drink will do---
Then lean back into your comfy chair
Take a wink or two---

I'M JUST A LITTLE RABBIT

I'm just a little rabbit that hides among the weeds.
I hear big old birds keep squawking that lives
among the trees.
My days are very simple, I'm as quiet as can be.
I can't help but believe they're looking for such
as me.
My fur is the color of the dead leaves from the trees.
But when the snow is falling, my fur turns snowy
white.
Then I run and play and hop, what a fairy delight.

THE TEACHING OF TIME

God teaches us to share.
Why not share a prayer?
He asks us to turn our hate into faith.
Sometimes we say, why worry, is there a hurry?
Yes, for example, we should have visions of a
Temple.
Let us stop the guessings,
Let us count our blessings.
Let us carry our Church in our heart.
Praise God he gave us a start.
Make us aware of his Spirit.
What a comforting thought to be near it.
There's no reason or rhythm,
Since the beginning of time.
As we ramble and roam, We shouldn't be content
until,
He calls us home.

A GIFT TO CHERISH
A.L.H. 1986

A troubled heart is like a visit from the dunes.
Like the universe, we keep seeking for other moons.
Let us turn back the memory of time.
When there was love and our hearts seem to chime.
We've discarded loves that we cherished.
Had we salvaged some to save a marriage.
Might we saved a heart ache or two.
Only God knows what we've been thru.
Sometimes we're sorry, sometimes not.
Now as we count our blessings,
We see what we've got.
Time on our hands and time to repent.
And thank God for the knowledge He's sent.

A TALK WITH GOD

God, You ask us to pray,
You ask us to obey,
You tell us we know not where we cometh,
Not where we goeth.
Then God answered thus:
Your life is compared to a rose.
As you struggled for life,
Your thought of unimportance,
Was at stake. You said; "how could I be
Important as a rose on a bush?"
You were crowded in the shadows,
Even engorged from the start.
You seem to know there was a meaning,
You carried in your heart.
As your pedals were unfolding,
And the sunshine peeped at you.
You knew you had a calling,
You had to carry thru.
Then I said, "How could I be noticed,
In this world that is so great?"
When there's so many that excel me,
In Honor, Love and Faith.

A VISITING ROSE

Then God said, "you can be a visiting rose."
Down God's pathway and share knowledge as
you go.
I've unfurled your pedals with special beauty.
But nip your statue to give you compassion and a
duty.
I've taught you love and to be loved.
I'll let you comfort your fellow men as you go.
I've trusted you to mend troubled hearts of people
that you know.
To comfort the down trodden and dry their tears.
To see sunlight thru clouds, that gather thru the
years.
As I leave a path on this earth,
I look back and still wonder,
What is my worth?

A THOUGHT

Be grateful for all the friends we've gathered,
To help us endure the storms we have weathered.

FLYING HALF MAST

A.L.H. 1986

Childhood dreams is often scoffed, it seems
To watch a bird build their nest,
One leaf or straw at a time, but they choose the best.
In looking for a mate, it's life time in their wake.
They bill and coo to find out who's who.
A commitment is forever, as though they knew.
As we choose our mate.
We also have dreams we relate.
Oh God, could our home be blessed with trust.
And escape the disgrace of lust?
Should we ignore the wayward thought?
Discard the danger of what nots,
To turn back, is to say, we are wrong.
But that's Gods way of getting along.
Is it because your pride won't let you?
Or your stride of life can't touch us?
Compare it to a wild goose chase,
Sometimes it ends up in empty waste.

DEPRESSION DAYS

True experiences.

When I sit in my study bettering ninety,
I'm alone with my thoughts.
They play games, other times resting quietly.
A memory comes to mind, thoughts entwined.
Should I share a heart felt time?
It's so vivid as it comes alive.
Depression was so hard to survive.
The food was a bargain, bread 5 cents a loaf.
Hamburger 10 cents a pound,
no butter you would know.
Coal was gathered along the tracks.
If we had gas to go to the desert for sage brush,
That's the fact.
We were glad to sew and make over our clothes.
The flour sacks were pretty designs for shirts
And dresses.
We made home brew and drank that too.
We had so many stamps for meat and sugar.
We canned fruit without sugar.
Would you believe we were happy?
The songs were happy. "Happy Days are here again."
Just a bit of depression days.

THE AWAKENING OF SPRINGTIME

The bees are making honey in the sycamore trees.
The birds are nesting, waiting for their families.
The blossoms on the fruit trees,
Praying for the cold freezes to cease.
Birds a winging their way to the blossoms,
Oh, so sweet.
They know ever lasting life will return to repeat.
Mushrooms are still asleep beneath the sod.
They too know God will awaken them, to give a nod.
We must have faith to know,
Our favorite frost will awaken and show.
Yes, God promises us everlasting life.
We must believe we will be revived.
Re-lived with newest faith,
And spiritual belief to claim with pride.

TIME ON YOUR HANDS

There seems to be no need,
If we care to take heed.
Why not join the morning crew,
Find out what they do.
A brisk walk will tell you lots.
While the morning dew sparkles on the walks.
You will find the birds are singing,
Could it be to comfort you?
Or is it because the day is new?
As the day wears on---Could there be a shut-in
That needs a call?
There is a time we should stretch tall.
Put a brush in your hand and look for cob webs
on the wall.
Please don't forget about your tummy,
You may find simple food really yummy.
Your personal hobby can be a friend,
Amuse and satisfy you to no end.
Read articles that are of interest to you.
Makes you a conversation piece, crisp and new.
Give the gossip seat a rest,
You will find it changes our day for the best.
Take it for granted, the best is before 10 p.m.
When you close your day,
Take an analysis and be prepared to say,
This has been a comforting, memorable day.

AN ARTIST'S BRUSH MAGIC

An artist's brush can soothe the soul,
Or rile our thoughts to points untold.
They let us travel with shades of blue,
Or dulls the horizon to give it a hue.
You look at pictures of places you've never been.
If it was any prettier it would be a sin.
It's the artist reflection, you'll agree.
You see through their eyes what may be.
It could be spiritual or uplifting or beauty.
That catches our eye, sometimes with risky
nudity.
Color is the scheme, blue can cause us to dream.
Yellow, the reflection of the sunshine, brings
Comfort to most everyone, sometime.
After all we must see he makes the brush behave
To the fifth degree.
Then there's purple, a mixed emotion.
With brightness dimmed, to cause us to see.
To meditate for what ever may be.
Red builds our hopes and brightens our day.
It lightens our burdens, what comes what may.
Long after the artist is faded and done,
Their work's still flourish as time goes on.
Many an artist as they flounder on and on,
Rarely a praise until they're gone.

I FEEL LIKE A KID AGAIN

An imaginary dream, I claim it for my very own.
I watch the children skip and play.
And the clouds are magic in their way.
They gather up and break away,
A way to amuse me any time of day.
A morning sun rise with color to share,
With sailors warning known to fear.
As I nod off in my favorite chair,
A relaxing afternoon is only fair.
I dream of loved ones that's gone on.
There so relaxed and happy to carry on.
I confess, old time friends, I can not trace.
It puts an ounce of heart aches in place.
Feeling like a kid again, being a senior shut in.
I deserve the right to imagine and dream.
Know the comfort of living, like the end of a
rainbow.
Maybe even a Pot of Gold.

THEY SAY THERE'S MUSIC IN HEAVEN

To the hearts of the liven
It must be to better our thoughts.
Give us courage to lend to pleasantries given.
Memories of music lends a touch of gold.
To bring back the best of long ago.
The age of time live within to say,
Music played a part in the good old days.
The old pump organ rang out pretty and true.
Now some of the music is faded and dim,
Still the music can be played to comfort a whim.
Let's keep music in our hearts.
In heaven, let us be a part.

WHY, WHY, WHY

We seek the mystery of Heaven,
Not willing to wait till we know.
Our seven astronauts, their choice was given.
God's hand called them home.
Their interests were many,
And touched the people of many walks of life.
It awakens our thoughts,
And shook our emotions,
Like a terrific earth quake in it's strife.
Have we out grown our earth?
Or failed to appreciate it's worth?
I'm asking this question---
I can't see very far thru this smoke and fog that
rests on,
Spoiling the vegetation and adding to the acid rain.
But who are we to complain? We are all guilty.
We stoke our fire with plastic and paper,
With air so heavy, it poisons the vapor.
We can have millions, by the acre of virgin land.
Where not one step of man has been taken.
Could we have our oversight of what heaven
might be?
Could we find heaven on earth, and just let it be?
The flowers are Heavenly and so are the trees.
Couldn't we make it better by sowing more seeds?
We could sow seeds of kindness that grows into
faith.
We could use silence to meditate and not let
happiness wait.
It's here today to grow and grow if we will only say,
This earth could be here to stay.

THE FAITH OF GARDENS

When spring arrives it renews our faith in human lives.
We can't wait to till the soil and start the spring time toil.
We rake and scrape and smooth it up.
But here comes the Christmas Pup.
He's just having fun, and knows he's amusing
Our little son.
Now it's time for seeds.
As we plant, we pray there's no room for weeds.
We failed to notice the robins watched.
Sure enough the rain beat the seeds to the top.
The birds and bugs thought we'd set the scene,
And had a get together to pick them clean.
To our chagrin, they miss a few,
And a thrill it was to see them break thru.
The new lettuce so good and tender too.
The radish, crisp and crunchy grew.
The slugs moved in to enjoy the crop.
We pulled them all and stopped that Tommy rot.
The tomatoes flourished and the vines grew tall.
We prayed for a few ripe ones before the fall.
At last the crop turned red,
We stuffed ourselves till we felt well fed.
We ate zucchini till it came out of our ears.
We shared, canned, froze for the coming year.
You can take it or leave it, gardening is not all bad.
In fact it makes the most exciting summer one
Could of ever had.
We saved the seed, Dad showed the way.
No need to starve this day and age.
Gardeners are indispensable.

TWO POT BELLIED PIGS

Two pot bellied pigs gift wrapped for the trip,
With pink toe nails and bows on their tails.
They found them a name, but what a shame.
They were naughty, not as good as they claimed.
They upset their milk, claimed they wanted slop.
They didn't care for the music of Bach.
They ran away and went to the farm.
Found their mommy back in the barn.
October 1992

I NEVER KNEW TILL I LOST YOU

I never knew till I lost you.
I never knew till you said "good bye"
The sunshine would hide, just shine on the sly.
I cherish the memories we knew.
Our togetherness turned into years.
Only God could measure the tears,
But he sealed our love.
Gave us lessons to learn.
Plenty of courage to partake of.
You were needed on every turn.
My ring that I wear, still shines in my heart,
Like the North Star guiding,
The wise men from afar.

THERE'S A TIME TO DREAM

There's a time to dream and a time to pray.
Count our blessings, what more can I say?
There's a joy in living, and a pleasure in giving.
Even things we've set aside,
For years we've treasured to abide.
The old sewing machine, the pedals torn,
The old churn, had it's day, tired and worn.
The victor phonograph, called talking machine,
Beats the modern, that hollers and screams.
Speaking of clothes so modern and new,
We had some left over just as too too.
The old hobbled skirts, thing of the past.

WOODEN MAN

I had my picture taken with a wooden carved out man.
Dressed as a hunter with a sun kissed tan.
I felt so proud, he made me look so small.
A mustache gave him power, he stood straight and tall.
The old gun he carried had a trace of rust.
I felt he could shoot if he must.
Now I'm in my nineties, still clinging to his arm,
Protected from harm.
I feel safe with his picture by the door.
When you live alone you can't expect much more.

DO I BELIEVE?

How could we doubt the greatest super power?
They've given him names in every language,
Where there's flowers.
To share his love, we must admit.
To give and take us sparingly as of yet.
Just to be right is important, we think.
We listen to rumors and tighten our link.
Why search when we are so certain we couldn't
be wrong.
Why listen to sermons that go on and on?
Each church has a steeple to glisten and shine.
It's a joy to worship and claim it as mine.
Sometimes it's tarnished as time goes on.
Disagreement and trouble and great carrying on.
God walked in the sunshine with dust on his feet.
Born with the animals that lay at his feet.
He's showed us a way to be simple and plain.
Warned us that nicely could become nothing but
vain.
He gives us a lesson at each waking day.
Strewed with sunshine and shadows,
Still shows us the way.
He tightens our tensions and asks us to see.
The people around us could be worse off than we.
If we all traveled the same way in life.
It would be so congested and choked down with
strife.
Be thankful we're given the knowledge to know.
The pathway will lead to the place called home.
If we've sown seeds of kindness to brighten the
way.
We'll all reap the harvest what waits us some day.

GOD TOUCHED OUR HEARTS

God touched our hearts and joined our hands.
And ask us to live by his command.
Let the sunshine in our hearts last,
And fade the shadows of the past.
Show us light by stars at night.
Diminish the fears that could haunt us thru the years.
God, how we pray, Oh, how we pray.
That we have seen the light of day.
Cause only God can show the way,
And comfort us each coming day.
March 2, 1986.

WHAT IS LOVE ?

Could it be sharing or caring?
It's Gods way of working, even if we are shirking.
Love is used in many ways,
Sometime just for personal gains.
We're all in need of deep concern---
To recognize false love, we never learn.
Some use the word on ever turn with
Enough frivolous thoughts to burn.
True love will grow and grow.
If it comes from the heart we'll surely know.
For some it's hard to say "I love you."
Their vocabulary seem to run true,
Do they reason out I love myself so much?
How could I love you,
Please tell me if I'm wrong.
Sometimes I toy with the thought as I go along.
Maybe they are afraid to say,
"I love you," because it won't last.
Maybe it's like putting a character in a cast.
As actors we are very good.
We won't tip our hand as children would.
Why don't we let our heart talk?
In the path of life we walk.
Love can be determined as:
> Kind thoughts, caring, sharing,
> Or furnishing the needs of our loved one.
Why not reinstate your feelings by saying,
The three simple words---
I love you---if you mean it.
P.S. I love you for listening.

STRAWBERRY, LEMON, OR LIME

Strawberry, lemon or lime,
Just lay the flavor on the line.
Strawberry, lemon or lime,
I'll take my chances any time.
When orange blossoms begin to bloom,
Then I know you'll change your tune.
Strawberry, lemon or lime,
Say you'll be mine any time.
1971

THE POET

A walk with a poet brightens the sunlight.
When the sky is sprinkled with stars they entrance the night.
They use words that drift us back.
Causes us to dream of the things we lack.
When they look at a flower, they count the pedals of.
It causes us to see the beauty,
As the shadows claim the day we've loved.
Even the chirp of a bird can cause them to look.
And sit on a park bench and think of the money it took;
To gather beauty for each of us to see.
What a better place to come to meditate,
Just made for such as we.
In the garden, they've gathered roses world wide.
A perfect place for butterflies to persuade,
And sometimes to hide.
A poet watches the shadows change.
Loves to be melancholy even in the haze.
I love people so deep in thought,
Sometimes they could care less if you were there or not.
A poet writes the poems for us to read.
To comfort our thoughts if we will only heed.
I believe God gives them power,
To comfort us in our darkest hour.
Help us build our dreams.
Even make things come true, it seems,
And causes us to fall in love with life.
Conquer our mixed emotions,
gather our thoughts more precise.

WHY GOD MADE A SLUG

Why God made a slug to crawl upon the earth.
I keep on saying, I surely have my worth.
I know I'm just a pest, I eat food that's the best.
I hide in the daytime and come out at night.
Then eat and chew to my hearts delight.
The trail I leave is shimmery and bright.
I can paint pictures with wondrous skill.
And when you view them, they give you a thrill
November 1992

OUR BOISE PAINT THE TOWN

Our Boise paint the town,
Each year comes back around.
A visit to our homes is assume,
Just to meet the volunteers,
Is like sniffing springtime blossoms.
Not only the house gets a face lift,
The trim and doors get the drift.
The touch ups are waiting their turn.
The decks so shabby, indeed they yearn.
I noticed young people doing their best.
The youths come thru when they're put to the test.
Boise the beautiful wouldn't be, If it weren't for caring people, plain to see.
I say thank you, thank you from my heart.
Still wishing I could do my part.
Just adds to the joy of living!

SWAT THAT FLY

Swat that fly, if you miss, he'll be back again.
He likes sweets, I'm so sweet, waiting here is neat.
Sugar on the table, I'm standing by.
If he ever stops to light, it will be good-bye.

I PICTURE A WEDDING DAY IN MAY

I picture a Wedding day in May,
After the tulip time is spent.
April showers will lament,
They brought the beauty of the May time flowers.
The green leaves whisper thru the trees,
And flowers scent the gentle breeze.
Love affairs will blossom like the flowers.
Why can't we be in love in this magic hour.
I picture a Wedding bouquet,
Held next to your heart on that day.
I picture a promise we vowed for a start.
Let's pledge a promise to Heaven above.
Why can't we be in love.

FALLING IN LOVE

Falling in love with the shadows of night,
Looking for someone to call Mr. Right.
Falling, I'm falling in love.
I'm falling in love with someone.
Someone to kiss me good-night.
Someone to love me and care.
The time will be delightful once again and again.
I'm thankful for someone tonight.
I promise to make things seem right.
Falling in love seems so right.
Falling in love all over again.
Let us stay together,
Let's face the weather.

ANGELIC WINGS ARE WAITING

A replacement of five organs were given
To Julianna 5 years old.
Prayers were offered by multitudes,
Many and good wishes untold.
She stole our hearts, and often with faith and
patience,
We were sold.
She wore a smile contagious, and waved with pride.
She won us over far and wide.
If Heavens were in calling,
Angelic wings are in waiting.
Please God, she's the sweetest girl this side of
Heaven.
Let her stay and adorn.
Our pleasure, she brings joy.
So, when she showed up, a great musical was
borne.
A special little girl came to planet Earth.

I DREAM OF LOVE

I dream of love that never was,
With beauty hides in clouds above.
A rock where lovers, make their future plans.
To spend their lives in other lands.
No more bomb rumbles,
No more shell shock troubles.
A life of dreams, to fade into the twilight,
Of my schemes.

OLD MAN WINTER

Mrs. And Mr. Winter moved right into Idaho to stay.
Changed the scenery and brought the frosties with
them, and turned our Idaho from green to gray.
Our forests look like Christmas trees,
Frosted like a cake.
Our lakes are turned to crystals,
Where snow queens love to skate.
Mrs. And Mr. Winter moved right into Idaho to stay.
The April showers bring April flowers,
And the pussy willows say Meow.
When Johnny Jump-ups blossom,
The bears quit playing possum.
It's time to look for fishin' worms and how.
We'll get our gold pans ready to take along in case,
We get tired of fishin', there's gold all over the
place.
When April showers bring April flowers,
And the pussy willows say Meow.

The summer breezes chase away the sneezes,
Then we think that every things O.K.
When sun suits take the nation,
The least is the most creations.
Then we start to live, Oh happy day.
The stars are sprinkled thru the skies,
Light the parks at night.
And the moon plays peek-a-boo,
Are you coming out tonight?
The summer breezes chase away the sneezes,
Then we think every things O.K.

The scare crows in the garden,
If you're afraid, I beg your pardon.
The autumn leaves will soon start tumblin' down.
The witches look for spiders,
The cob webs help to guide her.
There's sure to be a few spooks hangin' round.
The Idaho potatoes are bigger than my head,
The days we spend a diggin' them, I sure do dread.
The scare crows in the garden,
If you're afraid, I beg your pardon.
The autumn leaves will soon start tumblin' down.
June 22, 1955

65

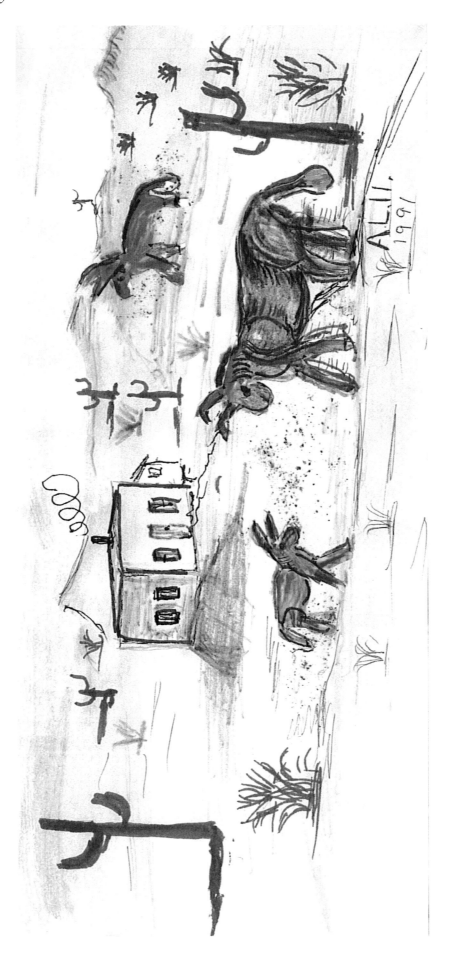

NEWS OF THE WEDDING

I sure hate this ol' dustin' and cleanin' and scrubbin'.
But do you know we're goin' to have a weddin' at
our house?
And Paw said "He was glad he was goin' to get rid
Of one mouth to feed."
And what more Paw said "he was gunnin' for that
stork;"
If he ever stops at our place, he'll get him too.
I did see a few strange feathers around the other day,
Do you suppose he did? I wonder?
Did you ever hear anybody propose? Don't you
dare tell,
But I heard it all. Was I ever uncomfortable.
I was standin' behind the old home-comfort
range;
When he right out and ask her to marry him.
Aunt Nellie had just stoked up the fire to finish
The bread bakin'.
I didn't dare let the love birds see me,
so I just sweat it out.
Elmer said, "Martha I love you as good as eerie
burrow I got".
I all ready bought you a weddin' present;
A brand new gold pan.
And with your big strong hands,
You can help me carry water to the slews box.
Then I heard Martha say, "Oh, Elmer."
Off stage voice; Times a wastin' and don't forget
To dust the piano.
And this is what Elmer sang;
I'll be seein' you this comin' fall.
June 22, 1955

HAVE MERCY

A broken hearted spirit, we have landed in our
hands.
Is this time for our forgiveness,
A soul is in waiting for his command.
Let the one's without forgiveness take their stand.
We are all God's people in wait.
Let us yield not into temptation for his sake.
A broken hearted spirit's life is so cold,
Especially when it's retold and retold.
Let us pray and pray and repray.
Oh please, have mercy on our fallin' spirits today.
September 10, 1998.

RAMBLING ROSES

Rambling Roses growing by the door.
Home Sweet Home keeps calling.
Braided carpets laying on the floor.
Calling Home Sweet Home for evermore.
I'd like a trip back home, I'd even walk back home.
I'll send a letter to tell them.
I'll hitch a ride back to the place that spells Home.
Just home sick, that's all.

GOOD AS GOLD CLUB

Have you heard about the good as gold club?
You should belong.
All you have to do is practice safety,
And promise to help your Mom.
What I saw down the street just made me stare;
The good as gold club couldn't bear to claim,
A member that lived there.
Toys scattered around the walk;
Wonder what they'd say if they could only talk?
The puppy was throwing the dolly about;
What will Santa say when he finds out?
One wheel was broken on Juniors bike,
The rain had been beating on Johnny's tricycle.
I pictured them all alive;
Then the bike spoke up and said,
"Why were we sent here to die?"
Nobody loves us, we might as well leave;
We're just misplaced toys sent here to grieve.
I would wheel, said the bike, but I'm too crippled up.
I'm just hoping, said the tricycle;
Someone will pick me up.
But the dolly murmured not a word;
She didn't even let on she heard.
But if she could have spoken,
 I'm sure she would have said;
"Where are all the pretty curls I once had on my
head."
My nakedness is showing; Oh God, please have
mercy.
Then I noticed the wind was blowing;
It hurled a wrapper off of a Hershey.
Over her face it clung like a shroud.
The leaves hovered closer and soon formed a
mound.
Soon to be forgotten like a worn out slave;
I guess she still lies in her shallow grave.
March 26, 1955.

WHO, WHO, I SAY

Who, stole the smile from the scarecrows lips?
And called for a witches brew?
Covered up the moon with a big black cloud.
"Who, Who," I said, "Who, Who."
A shadow and a spook were counting their loot.
When a magpie flew past to look.
He called a meeting for birds by the brook.
The owl recorded it in his little black book.
1970

THOUGHTS

There's all kinds of thoughts.
That visits us each day.
Sometimes we exaggerate the fear---
That comes and goes thru out the year.
Then again we'll cherish
The good thoughts that drift by.
And swear to goodness, happiness is
 Always nearby.
Oh well, life is a game.
Sometimes we lose, sometimes we win.
To dwell on what may have been, is just a sin.
What tomorrow brings, we can only guess.
Cherish the thought and God will take care of the rest.
Just try and think good thoughts-- that's the best.
June 1993

HARVESTING LEAVES

Harvest leaves in the Autumn breeze.
Watching the trees give up their leaves.
Walnuts to gather an Autumn Day.
Time to put Summer away.
Sweethearts are saying good-bye to Summer.
Nature's flowers have gone to slumber.
Spring comes along with their magic wands.
Touching and beauty responds.
Dream of that memory lane.
Linger and come back again.
Harvesting leaves in the Autumn breeze.
Time to put Summer away.
1973

MAMA'S TEARS

There are tears of joy,
When a new baby arrives,
Especially if it's a boy.

Then the first day of school,
There's tears again---
How will he act? Will the teacher like him?
Your heads in a spin.

He wants a bike, there he bumps and bruises.
But you take that in your stride.
But the motorcycle, you just can't abide.
Then again the tears you hide.

Time for the girls he might choose.
You settle for that, it's better than booze.

Then when you think she might take your son—
Oh God, I love him second to none.

When people say, She's such a pretty bride,
Then again the tears you shed are hard to hide.

But when the first Grandchild arrives,
There's tears of joy with bubbling pride!

AUGUST MOONLIGHT

Little mittens in the hay mow,
Playing hide and seek.
Little baby ducklings hiding close to Mama's feet.
Two shadows in the moonlight,
By the old wooden gate.
The August moon was traveling, as it was getting late.

August moonlight on a path so bright,
Leading to the water, where crickets chirp at night.
Weeping willows waving in the summer breeze.
Hoot owls calling softly from the old Oak trees.
August magic, August magic, August magic moon.
                                    1972

OH, WHAT A DAY.

Oh, What a day, Oh, What a day.
Sugar pops and chocolate drops,
And Kool-Aid just fresh made.
Fire crackers popping, how to celebrate the day.
We'll scare Tabby and aggravate Pa,
And give our Grandma nervous chills.
They'll soon be glad, to tell us we can go to
Strawberry Hill.
We'll glide around the hill side,
And whistle while we ride.
Decked in Red, White and Blue.
We'll ride fast and stop at the nicest shade and rest.
At last, then back.
We'll chase to the hamburger fry,
To watch the fire works shoot to the sky.
Oh, What a day!   1972

THE WHIMS OF THE IRISH VIOLINS

Like two nightingales in love,
Comes the whims of the Irish Violins.
Like a rumor of whispers sputter,
Like an outburst of spring time begins.

Pussy willows begin to bloom,
Johnny jump-ups will be here soon.
Robin Red Breasts are starting to spoon,
Echo's record their happy tunes.

I'm glad we decided on love,
Heard the whims of the Irish Violins.
When the wings of the love birds flutter,
Like an out burst of Spring begins.

GOOD THOUGHTS

I send good thoughts,
I vent my feelings to one and all,
Who's needing brighter days.
The clouds bring rain,
The rain brings flowers,
Flowers bring love,
And your prayers bring
Answers from above.
March 17, 1996.

LILACS IN APRIL

When the warm showers fall,
And the grass reaches tall.
There be a fragrance of lilacs in April.
When the clouds drift on by,
And the moon shines on high.
There be a fragrance of lilacs in April.
'Tis of you that I dream,
When I speak there's a beam.
Like a flickering light on a moon-lit stream.
With each season we'll share,
Down a pathway of cares,
The fragrance of lilacs in April. 1971

CHRISTMAS BACK HOME

Rice Plum Pudding in the pot.
Cranberry sauce will simmer and add color to
the lot.
The browning of the turkey to make the gravy lush.
To smell my Grandma's kitchen would
my greatest wish.

Christmas back home would be where I'd like to be.
I'm home for the clutter 'neath the tree.
I wonder if they miss the gifts I usually display.
Some day the folks back home will thank God,
For this given day.

The crackle of the parcels start at early dawn.
Some candy canes are missing,
And fresh tracks on the lawn.
Santa leaves a spirit that lasts thru out the year.
Christmas back home, I miss so much this year.
1970

THANKS FOR THE VALENTINE

Thanks for the valentine, I had a wonderful time.
Some day when we're grown-up, and you're
miles away.
I'll treasure the valentine, you gave me today.
[and he said] Two hearts entwine your name with
mine.
Valentine Sweetheart for-ever.
Then there'll be a time, when bells will chime.
I'll claim you for mine for-ever. 1966

THE TINKLE OF THE
NEW YEAR CHIMES

The clock strikes twelve,
The folks all sing Happy New Year all around.
The glasses tinkle happy times.
Let's all have another round.
Happy New Year, Happy times.
The tinkle of the New Year chimes.
Happy New Year, Happy times.
No one cares to stay in line.

The bells ring out, the people shout,
Happy New Year all around,
The horns blow loud, the musicians proud,
Play Old Lang Syne in our home town.
1971

CHRISTMAS TEDDY BEARS

I see the Christmas Teddy Bears.
Oodles of them everywhere,
With all the little boys and girls.
Hug and give them loving care.

My bear is almost seven years.
If he was lost, I'd be in salty tears.
He isn't quite as pretty, you can see,
But still rates high with me.
He lost an ear but we pinned it back.
I still love him, I can tell you that.

CIRCUS

We went to the circus and what did we see?
Elephants dancing and shaking their knees.
Girls were swinging high up in the tent.
Boys were catching them, they better you bet.
The band was playing and I sat close.
I loved their music, couldn't bear to miss a note.
Just then they called, a panther was loose.
He ran through the band right into a noose.
They still yelled, peanuts and popcorn,
real loud in my ear.
We cheered, laughed, clapped our hands,
Stuffed our tummy and we'll go back next year.
July 4, 1993

ASKING WHY?

When I heard you singing,
"The Call of the Wilds,"
Not a tear could I shed.
So I thought for awhile---
Why does God ask two people to care?
When there's hardly a symbol of love to share.
Are we selfish?
He taught us we couldn't forget.
And the togetherness we had, we shouldn't regret.
Time passes, that's true,
It goes on and on.
Like Cupids dart---It leaves a mar in the heart.

P.S. To my friend Verl November 1992

SPRING HAS ARRIVED

A little robin came to chirp, Hello.
She was rocking in the tree and testing out the
breeze.
Where could she build her nest?
She knew shade and safety would be the best.

She felt the fear of the cat, that was lurking below.
She looked in the eves for a nest that might
please.
Oh dear, the rain would wash her babies away.
So in an old oak tree the babies twittered with
glee.
And sang their little songs especially for me.
March 1993

A LITTLE RAT

A little rat who found a home.
They finely called him Sniffles.
So thankful, that a little boy,
Would take the care of Sniffles.
He listened every morning,
For the crackle of the box.
He even made a racket,
He's slyer than a fox.
If he could talk, he'd tell us,
I love this little boy.
I love my home and care he gives.
It brings me greatest joy.

71

FOR YOU AND FOR ME

Let's go for a walk, to see what we can see.
The sky is blue, the ocean too.
I'll bet the birds will sing for me and you.
There was a little cricket, he chirped the whole
night thru.
The Old Hoot Owl has hooted thru the night too.
Let's look for rocks flecked with gold.
This will be the best story ever told.
September 1992.

PRAISE AND LOVE HIM SECOND TO NONE
November 1992

In the quiet of my study, I ask God,
"Should I submit to things I don't believe?"
Should I go on pretending,
To gain the things I could achieve?
The things that seem to test me,
When they take a one way street.
As we travel down God's pathway,
There's stones, rocks and stickers to get into our
feet.
There must be rain and sunshine,
In everybody's life,
To give us insight and empathy,
To see the strife of life.
When things are great we say,
"Oh, Thank you God"
When the chips are down, to say with a frown,
"Oh God, have you forgot?"
Let's just be human, and take life as it comes,
And God, will take care of everyone.
Who praises and loves him second to none.

THE ELEPHANT'S EAR

A little bird hitched a ride on an elephant's ear.
Everything was great without a fear.
All at once a bug showed up, bite the elephant's
ear.
She shook her head, fanned her ears.
The bird was beat to a pulp, and could only say;
If it's the end of the world,
God, please give me time to pray.

WHAT CHANGE AT 89 YEARS

What could I be at 89?
I could be a clinging vine.
You would have to have someone that cares.
Perish the thought, there's no one there.
I can still read the news or watch T.V.
Sometimes I send a little write-up,
To remind the editor, there's still a me.
I'm not in the fast lane.
Seniors are alive and anxious to please.
Just ask me for a recipe,
I'll search until I know.
I wish I'd questioned Grandmother more,
When she ran the show.
Her knowledge was so precious, little did I know.
Her mind kept on a ticking, tho her footsteps
Seemed so slow.
Bygones are bygones---
I'm so thankful I've been spared,
I'm in the sun-set of life.
When the sun goes down,
Will my worth be declared?
April 1996 P.S. Would you rather be a statue or a
bird?

`THE CALL OF THE WILDS

You taught me the meaning of love,
Someday you will understand.
The Call of the Wilds are in command.
I needed your love to carry me thru.
The loving words I told you, still ring true.
I'll be on my way to explore the unknown new.
To know the meaning of love,
Was worth the time I spent with you.
P.S. Written for Verl Potts. November 22, 1992.

SQUIRREL

A little squirrel fell from a tree,
As clever as I am, it shouldn't happen to me.
My bones just ached and Mama said,
"You got to be careful, or you could be dead."
A big dog chased me and a black cat too.
I was just too fast and waved my tail.
And said "I'm safe at last.

THE RETIRED FISHERMAN

I sold some of my fishing' poles, and put away the rest.
I keep thinkin' these old legs will rest---
And I'll be back to do my best.
Just keep staring at my fishin' hat,
Wondering what to do with that.
It still has a silvery sheen,
It just can't end up never to be seen.
I could hang it on the wall,
And remember the fishin' tails I told that were
Pretty tall.
I could turn it upside down, and use it
for artificial flowers.
Then again I might be a winner,
And make it back and catch a fish for dinner.
November 1992

THE FROG STORY

I'm a home made frog,
That was made long, long ago.
Painted kelly green,
With a satin silky sheen.
I sat on a doily, on a wicker antique stand.
And never dreamt I'd end up broken in a can.
How can someone still love me?
But to my rescue came my owner,
And mended me with glue.
I still have horrid scratches,
And not as good as new.
Now I set on display.
You can see what I've been thru.
Believe me this sad story is really true.
November 1992

THE OLD MOTHER HEN

The old mother hen clucked, clucked to her chicks.
Don't get lost or you'll be in a fix.
But who was I to mind my Mom---
So I cheeped along the last of the throng.
I tasted this and I tasted that,
And had to hide from a big black cat.
I heard Mom cluck, I came on back,
Got under her wing and that was that.
November 1992

JUST WONDERING

I never did believe,
The moon was made out of green cheese.
It was hard to agree, the world was square,
Just to please.
I looked at the stars, they seemed so far.
There must be something up there,
Where ever you are.
I've been to lots of mountain tops,
Saw the most beautiful settings,
And decided they were God's Celestial Crops.
The springtime in the deserts,
Are so beautiful to behold.
Then again, I knew God owned them,
I didn't have to be told.
And in Autumn, he puts the plants to sleep.
Covers them with crunchy leaves so cozy, warm
And neat.
To be revived, again and again, in the spring.
When the awakening, with the trumpet sounds,
And the dream of the Golden Gate is torn down,
Will we walk on air, find time to share?
Just wondering.
November 1992

JINGLE JANGLE JUNGLE JOE

Jingle Jangle Jungle Joe,
That's what I do from head to toe.
Alligator shoes, Pig skin gloves too,
Western tie with a diamond stud.
All dressed up, no where to go.
Just got word, my gal said no—
I rap in the morning, I rap at night.
Everybody listens, so that's all right.
Jingle, Jangle, Jungle Joe,
That's what I do from head to toe.

LITTLE BITS OF WISDOM

Plant a seed of happiness.
The easiest thing to find is fault.
Listen to the happiness of birds.
If you plant a good thought it will grow.
The spirit of today is the success of tomorrow.
Pray for wisdom, strength in compassion.

OLD WOODEN MAN

I opened my gift and what did I see,
An old wooden man standing by me.
Idaho City came to mind.
I knew I would never leave the memories behind.
The shoot-out was exciting, and the ice cream
inviting.
Needless to say--- To be with you and Gwen,
Was the joy of the day.

A DOGGIE OUT ON THE RANGE

A little calf is called a doggie out on the range.
He jumps and plays and enjoys the freedom.
That's how he spends his days.
When the sun goes down and the moon comes up,
When the coyotes howl and the hoot owls hoot
hoot hoot.
He's close to his mommy, you can bet your boots.

MOUNTAIN VACATIONS

Mice can run, Snakes just crawl.
Giraffe are all very tall,
To eat the leaves high on the trees.
Bears can roll right down a hill, that's their skill.
They eat huckleberries, like you and me.
They can even climb a tree.
So in the woods remember you are visiting.
That's where they live.
Ham and bacon, that's their treat,
Keep your camp clean and neat.
September 1994

CHRISTMAS LIGHTS

Christmas lights are beautiful,
When you have a home with Mom and Dad.
You know there are little girls and boys,
That doesn't have a home, it's sad.
You can only see the pretty lights,
When they're on the street at night.
If God loves them as much as me,
Please, God, let them have a pretty tree,
With good things to eat, like me.

BABY FROG

Baby frog came to my house,
To get a drink of water.
He was afraid of a big magpie,
For that he'd be slaughtered.
Sure enough, the old magpie
When the frog was leaving
Flew down from the Apple tree.
The frog said, "He grabbed a rock,
Instead of me."
November 1992

A LITTLE BIRD THAT FLEW AWAY

The nest was full of birdies.
There were five of us in fact.
Our Mama brought us worms each day,
And divided, so they say.
Mine were always skimpy,
I was the tail end of the lot.
So I flew away to the west,
When night came I had no nest.
I was cold and hungry, too.
When I got back, I said, "Mama guess Who?"

LIFES MYSTERY CUP

After 88 years I've summed it up.
I've drank the bitter and the sweet out of life's
Mystery cup.
I've had my ups and my downs,
Spent time just clowning round.
I've skimped and saved and tried to pretend,
I'm practical and logical right to the end.
I hang on to keepsakes and even old clothes.
Sew and remodel until goodness knows.
I buy old dolls forlorn and unwanted,
Redress them, caress them and give them a home.
People wonder what makes me tick,
I just look forward to what comes next.
My Life has been a wonder, I've made it so.
New things happen where ever I go.
I live for the minute, cause I've spent the past.
It's up to my maker, how long I will last.
July 28, 1995

McKINNEY CHRISTMAS 1994

T'was the night before Christmas and all thru the house,
Not a creature was stirring, not even the rat.
The cats were cuddled on the sofa to watch,
They knew things would happen, so their eyes didn't bat.
They heard tiny foot steps. Who could that be,
David just checking the lights on the tree.
There was Michael dreaming of things that might be.
Oh, golly, maybe a computer for me.
There was Mary bemoaning the fact,
She couldn't finish the things she started,
That were still in tact.
Well Mackey, had given in to accepting the things,
Finally decided no way to win.
Then all of a sudden a clatter was heard.
David screamed and hollered and gave them the word.
They were all in their night caps, a sight to be seen.
Santa had been there and left all the things.
Could they find any thing that really pleased?
He even left Sniffles a piece of cheese.

A SNOW FLAKE

A snow flake is like a thought when it first arrived.
It's undecided where to land,
As it gathers company, they stick together.
And things start to be as tho in command.
A thought turns into an idea, an idea turns into a project.
A project turns into many permanent things.
Let our thoughts work miracles, they're so
Precious to own.
You will find there's a way.
To evaluate them when they're full grown.

NOVEMBER 1995

Leaves almost down, dancing and skipping to and fro.
Spring bulbs are planted to bring a spring time show.
Yes, grapes have filled the air with an aroma you can't Believe.
To whet an appetite of young and old.
We'll ask for a sample, adding please for a place to call
"Home Sweet Home."
Turkey, Sweet potatoes and Pumpkin pie,
Will say it every time.

INVADED WITH LEAF RAKERS

One frosty November cold morning
I was invaded with leaf rakers.
Thirteen to be exact.
I smiled and waved my cane,
Did everything but complain.
It rumbled in my mind,
There's still many people that are kind.
It's so up lifting to a shut-in,
To know people really care.
And enjoy the tidiness we've once known.
I could have just said "Thank You"
And let it go at that point.
When I count my blessings, I believe
There's not a helping hand missing,
That God doesn't bless!

THE WORLD IN 1993

This is the world in 1993.
As I ponder what have I achieved?
I've fought my way for eighty six years.
Thru sunshine, rain, happiness and tears.
In my beginning, horses were our speed.
A car just now and then is all could meet,
As they thickened every one knew,
Like a bad weed, they grew and grew.
The train riding from time to time.
Was such a joy and considered sublime.
Then they took a back seat.
We thought the airplane would be complete,
Now we talk of the speed of light.
It chills my heart with a bit of fright.
They speak of Armageddon to tear up the world,
So they can have something new and ruin it too.
We recycle, take old things and make new.
But still want to discard our earth like an old shoe.
Churches and religions are thick and fast.
They change their beliefs, cause they just can't last.
Times are changing and they must change too
The free thinkers are starting to sift it thru.
There's more than one way,
God intended us to stay---
Think things thru, it's the best you can do.

TO STAY ALIVE AT 85

To stay alive at eighty five---
It's not what you call, Jump and Jive---

You look for your shoes, of course one is gone.
Well, what's the difference if they don't match,
You can still get along---
You go to the bathroom and look in the mirror,
Who shinned that glass and left that smear?
You look for your teeth and they're not there.
They were put to soak, but the container was bare.
You spittered and cussed, you knew you were right.
Sure enough I'd slept with them in my mouth
All night.

I went to the kitchen to get some food,
Oh, why bother, a crust of bread will do.
You turn on the T.V. and what do you hear?
You're headed for Hell and Damnation,
If you don't start to fear.

California is to drop in the sea, Idaho is next.
Maybe it could be, so I turned that off.
Picked up the phone, called, what was called,
shut-ins.
No body was home. I lifted the blinds and discovered
Sunshine. Read in the paper we are getting a raise.
A friend called to take me to dinner with friends.
I puffed up my hair, powdered my face,
Found the mate to my shoe.
Put a smile on my face, cause I was a winner.
I enjoyed the outing thru and thru.

When you're down, there is only one way to go.
Lift your spirits and go up.
November 1992

IF I WERE A KID AGAIN

If I were a kid again---Garden Project.
I'd drown the weeds, plant the seeds.
Let rain drops fall.
Give the watermelon an extra drink,
Let the broccoli wait.
Fourth of July, chickens big enough to fry.
The goodies Mom and Sister make, takes the cake.
We'll ride the ponies, the monies, if they come in
first

CANADIAN BACK COUNTRY

I listened to the coyotes howl,
As I rode the back country trail.
We listened for the cow bells,
That would tinkle without fail.
But who's were who, and what was what?
You had to recognize them on the spot.
My cutting horse was Trumpet up too,
I gave him credit for what he knew.
So I knew to lay flat on my belly,
And prayed for a gulley,
Cause I've been brushed off like a horse fly.
I just can't deny, Life on the Canadian homestead!
April 2, 1996

THE OLD HOMESTEAD IN CANADA

We lived by a lake, the water was great..
It was quack, quack in the morning,
quack, quack at night.
In the evening a mud hen's delight.
At the break of dawn, the rooster crowed.
Get ready for school was all I knowed.
I saddled my pony and took down the road.
Made up my songs as I went along.
One of the memories of long ago.

IRISH JOKES

The traditions of Irish Jokes,
Were enjoyed by home time folks.
Green was sure to be in place,
Even if only as a shoe lace.
Corn beef and cabbage, cooked to a numbens
To taste.
An Irish stew can come thru,
For the family to enjoy, too.
Let Grandpa tell about the leprechauns.
Grandma talked about the goin' ons.
Irish music touched our hearts.
The Wild Irish Rose took a part.
I'll be with you in Apple Blossom Time,
Reserved for parties of Irish Chime.
Fiddlers whipped up a jig,
Whipped up the party.
We all went home jolly and happy. 1999

CHANTING ABOUT THE BY-GONE DAYS
September 1998

We chant about the by-gone days.
There's bitter and the sweet in many ways.
When we reach the sunset of life,
There's too many things to tell to be polite.
Sweet sixteen was always a high light.
Surely now, to get more secrets would be right.
Just to get a corset and cinch it up.
Put on a brassiere with nothing to prop up.
If we had a sweetheart that would go away,
We could write little love letters, what to say?
My girl friends used to talk about the do's and don'ts.
I didn't even know the will's and won'ts.
I pretended I was in on all the do's and don'ts.
A little piece of wedding cake under the pillow,
Was suppose to let us dream of our future fellow.
Now girl's I told the story.
Grandma's dreams were future glory.

FATHERS DAY

Fathers day is coming soon.
Take time out to say you knew.
Even if he's laid to rest.
Memories so dear is best.
It's his day, ask friends to listen
To what you have to say.
I loved him with all my heart.
I couldn't picture to be apart.
He was my strength.
Our music joined into solid gratitude.
Spirit comfort is by my side.
It still whispers, it grew.
Love ya, Papa, if you only knew.

THE FALLING OF THE LEAVES

The falling of the leaves.
They are as crisp as the breeze.
Box Elder leaves dancing from the trees,
Forming blankets around the plants,
So the chill of winter won't have a chance.

The goblins and witches are busy,
Sewing their costumes that need fixing.
Some will be pretty ghosts from the past.
Shining jewels of Kings and Queens of the past.
The most fun of all, yell trick or treat.
Ring the door bell to see who you will meet.

GOD HAS HIS HELPERS

God has his helpers, I often wonder who?
We all complain about bad hair do's,
When we think nobody cares.
Here comes loved ones and friends,
To let us know they care.
I write little notes and say, Thank You,
I'm glad you are there. A phone call can be so neat.
Really a day time treat.
Living alone with one and only,
Loved ones and friends is what we depend.
Don't give up, to keep life worth living.
My heart still beats at the old time rate.
The rumble of the rhythm clicks time out,
we should debate.
Stay on line, keep on time,
Don't let progress wreck the line.
Don't let the time wreck the minute.
Don't turn time progress to the Senate.
Still take four steps to the march.
Waltz to three quarter time.
Let gossip, music keep our heart sublime.
Submit to discipline, there's still time.

MOTHER'S DAY

When I chose a card for you,
I look them thru and thru,
Nothing seems to really fit "except"
You've been a Wonderful Mother to me.

Mother, down thru the years you've dried my tears,
Comforted me and lessened my cares.
You made me understand that,
Power and strength is at one's command,
I hope I never let you down.

Mother, you taught me that a frown is
A smile turned upside down,
And close enough that it would be easy found.

TO STAY ALIVE AT 86

To stay alive at 86, you might say it's full of tricks.
When you crawl out of bed with aches and pains,
Don't blame it on your age, just say it's the rains.
When you write in your diary, keep it smooth.
Say everything's O.K. What can you lose?
Don't let on old age is a drag.
Let on you do more, even tho it's just a brag.
Think of somebody to call, worse off than you.
It will pep you up even if you knew,
That they are going to dinner and you were
eating stew.
God. Must love us to let us live,
So always save the best thoughts to give.
June 1993

DEE'S BIRTHDAY
October 7, 1999

While a way a dream, that lingers in my heart.
A new day, sunshine, a sparkle in my heart to call
mine.
Enjoy each day, flowers if they may.
Wish upon a wish, could come back to stay.
And not refill a dream, where your dream loves to
play.
Listen to the birds sing, as they build their baby
nests.
Next year a nest, new hopes to come their way.
Let faith fill your heart each day.

CHANGING OF TIMES 1993

When I was a kid, we wore button shoes,
Lace on our petticoats, skirts to our shoe tops too.
We had long hair, hard to comb.
They let it loose for the Christmas play.
Braided it back, when we got home.
Then came the flapper age, of course short skirts
were all the rage. We bobbed our hair.
Skirts on the bias was a real flare.
Eye make-up was something new.
Harold Lloyd glass, we wore them too.
Then in the thirties we lowered our skirts.
Wore peaked toed shoes, till our feet really hurt.
In the forties we slowed up the music, and danced
Cheek to cheek. Closer and closer,
If you told, you were a sneak!
In the fifties, I just couldn't compete.
Sloppy shoes and sweat shirts, anything but neat.
The girls started complaining, Why don't I rate?
The boys couldn't help to make a complaint.
Then came the "pill," they submitted to will.
They would be popular, to these chagrin, they
were still.
They worried, with reason. Things weren't the same.
But what could they do, who was to blame?
They've limped into their 30's and never dressed up.
The names for their babies are never brought up.
Women lib has taken a stride.
They are missing the day they could be a bride.
The men are taking their way of life.
They're missing the home, their Fathers whole
pride.
Surely there's a God in Heaven, that's looking
down.
I can't help but believe, he's wearing a frown.

DADDY AND MAME

Daddy and Mame went out on the town.
That's when I was found.
That's when the blame went round and round.
No-body went around and took the blame.
When I thought of it, Oh, what a shame!
I'll wear a smile, act real chipper,
Liven up a party stardom, a secret dipper.
In happy thoughts, I took pride.
My joy was hard to hide.
Twinkling my guide, family enjoyed in their stride.
Sent to abide, Thank you, God.

TELL IT LIKE IT WAS

Monday use to be; The wash day.
Now we find it just like play.
Tuesday we sprinkled the clothes,
Now we iron when, who knows?
Wednesday; we mended the clothes,
That ripped and broke.
Thursday we read and answered the mail.
We also burnt the mail.
Friday; Plan the weekend.
Plan the menu, give each one what to do.
Saturday, shop, bake, clean, hold your cool,
Don't get mean.
Sunday; early to church, be packed, gather pets,
Take off for best bet!

I BELIEVE IN CHRISTMAS

I believe in Christmas.
Happiness is a plus.
Get the card list ready,
Always add a few new.
The memories of the loved ones,
Gone on to resting.
Put up the lights, they are such a delight.
Add new thing to make them bright.
For a new cheer, give Santa a new beard.
Fill the sleigh with holly,
Pretend we are all jolly.
Leave a note on the tree,
Give them a treat for me.
I'll fix the dinner,
Have mistletoe where they enter.
Music is a tradition.
The joy of singing is a religion.
Merry Christmas for everyone, a mission of
Happy Good Tidings to All.

MOMBOA NO. 5

Learn to dance mambo no. 5.
First you wiggle and then wag.
Take a partner or try it stag.
Mind over matter,
Real live music or just a platter.
A real trick, shine your shoes.
Wax your hair, what you got to lose?
Take a wall flower, act like you care.
Your time of your life,
You'll remember it, I swear.

ALL I ASK

All I ask in 2000, the same old moon,
We can cuddle 'neath.
The stars sprinkling then a usual bit of quest.
The starting of a new year,
Best of all, a promise of progress for all.
Let February be full of hearts,
Sent to have a ball, even chocolate candy,
To enjoy with faith, we can manage.
In advance Happy Birthday, everyone.
Even in 2000, will be Home Spun.

DOING WHAT COMES NATURALLY

Doing what comes naturally, suits me to a tea.
If I want, have my way, I think it's up to me.
Open up the blinds if the sun shines.
If it's storming, take your time.
When the phone rings, find out who's on line.
If you don't answer, I'll save a dime.
I wonder from time to time, If I'd answered,
A nice dinner could have been mine.
Oh, Well!

CHRISTMAS EVE

Let us ride with Santa, Christmas Eve.
Be ready early, sneak on his load early.
Sister, you and I, will finely see,
He has to travel by light of speed.
We'll check his list for you and me.
Over the roof tops, down the lanes,
Into homes thru window panes.
Music playing.
Thank you, Santa, when he was thru.
Thank you , Santa, for Sis and me.
The trip so magic, just to see.

QUIET ZONE

Shades of night, purple shadows delight.
A night bird calling for his mate.
Then to love would be so great,
The honeymooners in the month of June.
Loved their favorite Quiet Zone.
The hoot owl knew the time was for the Quiet
Zone.
Lovers lane was in the Quiet Zone.
Daring as it seems, the moon could beam,
Not a shadow moved.

GUESS WHO

Aunts that love to tell amusing stories,
And have a comfy way to chat.
You can feel she will listen close,
When you tell her this and that.
Aunts make you feel important,
Let you grow up in time.
When you feel lonely,
She will claim you for mine.
Really like a friend and a second Mom.
Listens to your troubles,
With a comforting way of charm.

KEY FOR THOSE WHO BELIEVE

Early as the days that pass,
If we live as things passed,
Knowing and believing , we will be receiving
Blessings given as thy gift and exist.
Two down trodden lives as a missed gift.
Better days are waiting, you will find for the
taking.
Look for the sun that shines on the mountain.
It's winning it's way, you can count.
We should bless and be blessed,
And a day of rest for those, who believe, will
receive.
May 9, 1999

YAH WHO, WHO YAH

Chants of guess who, A friendly chant to guess
who,
On the plains of old Wyoming.
A camp made up of boxes, huddled 'neath
the Wyoming moon.
Welcome to the western culture,
Warning of the wilder vulture,
back to the friendly chant.
Yah Who, Who Yah, Who Yah.
The howl of the wolves, the hoot owls too,
Campers huddle closer, "neath the western moon.

I WONDER WHO?

I wonder who could make us happy?
Shine our shoes, lay out the news.
Let us listen to what we choose.
Never refuse to bake a cake,
For a fishin' trip he planned to make.
Take the family car to a game.
A church outing you'd planned.
I admit I love that man!
Pray to God, what more can I stand.
A brand new car, let me live where we are.
Visit our children and a family reunion every year.

THOUGHTS

Thoughts can be good, be returned with splendor.
Thoughts can be cruel, returned sad as a rule.
Don't abide with ugly thoughts, lend good
thoughts.
Repeat good thoughts, recycle good thoughts.
When the day is over, count your good thoughts.
Count them as blessings
Note: send good thoughts, write them down,
You'll be surprised, how long they'll hang
around.

SUNSET

There's a sunset waiting,
 for autumn leaves are beginning to fall.
Their life is not over, springtime back
for their take over.
Fresh and green for a spring time scene.
We've been promised ever lasting life.
Summer time carries a summer glow.
We replenish our veggies, one would know.
The harvest moon brings romantic loons.
Young folks hum romantic tunes.
Back to the slopes to ski and play.
Winter is here to stay, come what may.

NATURE

When nature hands you a downer,
Use your power for an upper.
There's a ladder to success,
Don't try for the top.
Just ride the waves but not stop.
Every day brings ideas, bright and new.
Check the books, find out who's who.
Sometimes I wonder if fine print,
Isn't sent, a notice, to take a hint.

WHO HAA, HAA WHO

Who Haa, we are on a roll.
Pay no attention, who knows.
They even aimed at the moon.
Tell us our homes will no more soon.
I listen to the birds singing in the spring.
Noticed the snow birds on the wing.
Snow melting, disappearing,
Spring preparing for new.
Who Haa, Who Haa.
Still things left to do.

A ROCK-A-BYE MOON

A rock-a-bye moon has a message, that's true.
Slow down rhythm, listen to the whisper in your ear.
Tender love, music, back and near.
Now's the time, time is wasting'.
You can advance, start bragging'.
Dad promised a rose garden,
He didn't even have a garden.
Mom, promised him me. What I was to see.
Now we are a Family Tree.
A promise you couldn't believe.
A life after 2000, wait and see.

SMILE

A smile sends a message, to someone feeling down.
Sweetens the rain clouds hangin' round.
Tell your pets you love them.
To stay with me is, I recommend.
Rain clouds freshens the air.
Flowers need rain drop care.
A frown is a smile, upside down.

DOWN BY THE OLD SWIMMIN' HOLE

Down by the old swimmin' hole,
Where I first met you.
A good time party for one and all.
A smoldering camp fire,
Waiting for a food hour.
Our back to school, reciting the golden rule.
We bowed our heads, our missed pals, what a dread.
I still have a soul, I met at the old swimmin' hole.

MY DREAM CAME TRUE

My dream came true when I found you.
Things never happened like the love stories, I
knew.
Three more years of school,
School nights were a study rule.
A year went by, still had my guy.
Once a week date, I wondered why.
We got together, it seems.
You had to study, play themes.
Dating can be your dream.
If it never comes true,
Should I think of something else to do?
Just go out, find something new.

WHEN MOM WAS CALLED HOME

Time lingers, when Mom's gone.
When her worldly chores are done.
She is called for duties beyond on a misty morn.
There the flowers tossing in the breeze and carry
on.
The folded, mended clothes she hung with pride.
So neat, her mending to hide.
When we kneel to pray,
We ask, it's too much to ask her to stay.
Pray for us if you may,
when we're called home on our day.

ROLL UP THE RUG

A gate swings both ways.
If it's stormy, there'll be better days.
Shine up your shoes, what you got to loose?
Brush the clouds away.
The old banjo, covered with dust..
Shine it up, check the strings for rust.
Call your buddies, time to play.
Some popcorn rhythm would be nice.
Roll up the rug, give a man a hug.
Even Grandma could get the bug.
Gramps a tuning up the fiddle,
When music's on, he's in the middle.
Auntie Alice plays popcorn rhythm.
Might sing a little, if not forbidden.
April 1999

MOTHERS DAY SOON

If I were a kid again, I'd tell her how I loved her.
The cookies she baked, I prefer.
She taught me to share, no matter when or where.
She let me choose the material for our clothes.
When I chose the horse shoes on the red,
The sales ladies coaxed her to let me have it.
Now my choice, I could hear a definite dread.
She's been gone since 1915.
Her comforting voice guides my thoughts and ways.
Her Heavenly Ways still obeys.
1999

IDAHO ROCKY MOUNTAIN MOON

Idaho rocky mountain moon, peekin' down the
canyon.
Lookin' for the shadows coming soon.
Of adopted wolves, finding a home to hide till
noon.
When the moon goes down and the sun comes up.
And the farmers work starts up.
The trusty dogs have work to do.
Wolves will look else where before they're thru.
Live in harmony, give and take.
Find a new home at stake.
May 1999

IF MY MEMORY SERVES ME RIGHT

If my memory serves me right,
It was a moonlight night.
Fireflies darting, dancing, creating magic
moonlight.
Night birds, like the whippoorwill,
looked down from above.
The breeze stood still.
My heart stood still, but witnessed a thrill.
If there was harmony left in the world.
We could have peace, harmony unfurled.
Peace on Earth adorns our Faith.
God's Promise, worth the wait.
Praise the wait, praise the wait.
Not too late, Praise Him for the Wait.

FOLLOW YOUR HEART

Come back to me, if she wants back, follow your
heart.
True love can always play a part.
Picture a Family waiting to be claimed.
A future waiting to happen.
A baby waiting to be named.
If you roamed, time for a home to call your own.
Paint Welcome on the gate before it's too late.
You are in charge.
June 10, 1999

SPRINGTIME FROLIC

Down by the meadow on Cow Creek,
The frogs kept music alive.
Mushrooms popped up, trying to hide.
Meadow larks building a home of pride.
Johnny jump-ups kissed by the morning dew.
Evening shadows bending down,
Time to bring in the milking cows.
Rovers trip with the milk maid.
Enjoying the nests he disturbed.
His worthiness is important aid.
Suppertime drawing near,
Ice Cream, this time of year.
Happy Valley Farm.
April 1999

MAY TIME

Year in and year out,
We keep faith the May flowers will be out.
Emeralds for the May Birthdays.
And lace the May Pole for plays.
Frogs chatter all night through.
Hoot owls hoot when they're thru.
Fire Flies are happy too,
Light their magic is what they say.
Dandelion harvest for brewing,
Sharing the pollen for the doing.
April showers brought the May Flowers.

1907---1999

A Birthday is a special day.
The June birthdays admire roses.
They burst into June blooms.
We are accused of dual personalities,
Maybe so, We are entertaining and exciting.
We love a laugh, sometimes laugh at love.
We have tears to spare, when trouble bubbles.
I love my June Bug friends.
I take this time to thank them and friends.
Showing so much kindness.
Forgive me for my short comings.
Always your Friend and Aunt Alice.

1949

I saved a piece of wedding cake.
It long ago has gone dry and stale.
Still welded tight with togetherness,
It wasn't-a-mistake.
Bits of dreams come and go,
But true love lets you know.
Side by side you still take pride,
In making quite a show.
Homes are built piece by piece.
To celebrate a Golden Wedding
Is so precious, I've been told.
A surviving certificate just to have and hold.
June 1999

SOMEONE

Someone to tell my troubles to,
Someone to listen to what's new.
Someone that brings joy to life.
Someone to spice up life.
If things are dull around,
Go out and find out what's hangin' round.

Moonlight madness they talk about---
False hope comes close when we are in doubt.
Happiness awaits till time to abate.
Your dream could be waiting, late to be your date.
April 14, 1999

MIDNIGHT MAGIC

Look up among the stars,
There's wonderment where ever you are.
They sprinkle dreams and love dreams from afar.
Magic can take a timelessness by far.
Secure a time for all.
When we travel the speed of light---
Be back home before the end of night.

PRAYER WHEEL

Give a prayer wheel a whirl.
Let it tell you what to do.
Lucky you, you'll know if it's your lucky day.
If not, give it a whirl another day.
A prayer wheel stands straight and tall.
Tempting, I admit, find out if you have the grit.
A message from a prayer wheel,
Has a message to reveal.

ANGEL VOICES

Angel voices drifting in the morning air.
Birds twittering and joining breezes fare.
Millennium waiting in the wings,
For 2000 to begin.
A farewell is like a security friend going away.
We must have faith, our faith is here to stay.
The moon, the stars, and sun will be unaware.
They'll be prepared to be on duty,
As Our Maker predicted.
1999---2000

BODY AND SOUL

Body and soul given to each one.
Our body is to respect and honor.
Mere our fellowmen on the same level.
Is it so important to know it all?
When the good book tells us,
We know not when we are called.
Stay close with caring,
Keep our love proud and tall.

UNCLE MUD HOG BROWN

Uncle Mud Hog Brown, known well all round town.
He loved life, he lived to eat and eat to live.
Uncle Mud Hog, an old time judge.
Had candy for the busy street.
A treat for the street kids, bets and town bids.
Uncle Mud Hog petted dogs.
Uncle Mud Hog even loved the southern fog.
Walked miles with his friendly dog.
Sunday morn the Church Bell rang.
Uncle Mud Hog opened and checked
to open the doors, and shined the floors.
Uncle Mud Hog shared his loop with home town folk,
With the love of Our Maker above.

POP CORN RHYTHM

Join the band with popcorn rhythm.
Slap the spoons with rhythm God given.
Shape them, wiggle them, just beat time.
The band will notice, you can add a chime.
It's all in fun, the joy to rhythm has begun.
The popcorns gone, the fun begun.
The only free thing in 1999 or 2000.
June 1999

BREAKFAST ON THE FARM

We listened close for the alarm.
Feeding cattle in the barn,
Roasters crowing to start the day.
Cattle ready to chow on hay.
Mom, was busy getting ready,
Smelling up the kitchen with biscuits and gravy.
A morning prayer was not a miss.
And Mom's wish with a good wish kiss.

Now go take on the day.

THE JOY OF WILD LIFE CAMP

Stitch your name inside your shoes.
Gather old knives, forks and spoons.
Take some old pots you want to loose.
Let Mom remind us what to do.
Leave the livin' to gather dust at home,
Such as dust, dirt, mildew and any clutter
That has moved in.
Gather up swimsuits, comfy boots, 'slippers.
Don't forget, Dad to drive, take us
to the swimmin' hole.
When Dad plays out, remember Mom can drive.
Safety too, when we arrive.
1999

GODS WAY OF LIVING

I loved the way he told me, I could be his bride.
Being alone and lonesome, I love to be by his
side.
If I were getting married, we would have to hide.
I wore my Mother's wedding ring,
Being married was the thing.
Home's were hard to come by,
house keeping could be tough,
Recycling pots, pans and dishes.
Found an empty house, that was enough.
True love has a real beginning.
God's way is guiding your way.
His vows protects your living.
Truly a Gods giving.

ALAMOSA CHRISTMAS TREE

Grandpa found an evergreen growing in debris.
He brought it home, hoping it could be
a Christmas tree.
Daddy sat it up, Mommy was happy too.
Sister strung the popcorn and hung it on the tree.
The brothers ate it off the strings.
Mom crocheted the strings into Angel Wings.
We made a wreath of Christmas Cards,
A greeting for our door.
Let Christmas live within our hearts.
Love for ever more.

SOUND OF WAR

A sound of war across the sea.
I must admit, it troubles me.
World War No #1 Armistice Day signed.
Never again comes to mind.
Some praised, some blamed us.
Oh, how we prayed, if we would keep our trust.
We've grown in size and power pride.
Keep in mind, we can lose in the bat of an eye.
Let Our Maker reign and bring us back our way
of life.
That will lesson our strife and bless us.

A BASKET OF ROSES

A basket of roses faded and gone.
A memory still lingers on.
A thrill still lives in my heart as time goes on.
Embers burning, low rekindled.
Rekindle a glow, if I find my lost love.
And receive a message from above.
Please God send back my love.
True love awaits, please not too late.

KEEP SAKE LOVE NOTES

Keepsake love notes yellow with age.
Smelly with mothballs, missing a page.
A secret I've carried in my heart.
Thinking of what might have been.
Pining bygones is a sin,
Find a new love, let life begin.
Let the leaves fall where they may.
Praise your up-beat days,
Smiles brings better ways.

UP BEAT PETE

Up Beat Pete, so neat.
Life's way, retreat,
When the sun goes down,
And the moon comes up.
Up Beat Pete was on retreat.
Some girl friends like a worn shoe.
Just take a look, that could be new.
The shock came when the hair turned gray.
He could turn that back and be ready to say,
Baby, the time has come to take on the day.
Sorry Honey, I'm too old to play.
Just Buzz and Buzz,
Brag about what you use to was.

DON'T SAY IT ISN'T SO

The magic of starlight stardom,
Dancing in a stardom dream.
Reality shook my dreams.
I awakened to see, was I special
Just cause it was me?
The answer is no.
An up-beat smile is worthwhile.
You can find diamonds in the sand.
A treasure can wear a brand.
I found a rainbow, Don't say it isn't so.

THE PROMISED LAND

The promised land at his command.
Troubles keeps brewing, warriors are ready.
Even tho hearts are heavy,
Why keep, get even on things long gone.
War that's long gone, a memory of a song.
Even then, breaking our heart's was wrong.
Armistice promises, been broken.
Now they find reason for a token.
Let turmoil cease, Let God, guide us to the land.
They call The Promised Land, at his command.

FUN FUN FUN

A birthday party, popcorn rhythm, is worth livin'.
It tickled the toes, is all the go, Heaven knows.
Pick a guy that grabs your hand,
That swings with the popcorn rhythm band.
Go to the beach, kick up the amber sand.
Sunset sparkles on mellow sand-dunes..
Call it a day, A Happy Birthday.
Till A Happy Birthday comes back another day.

BRING ON THE SUNSHINE

Bring on the sunshine and talk about the weather.
When the clouds roll in, visiting raindrops will gather.
Drooping Sun Flowers lift their heads.
They need their seeds for future beds.
Birds chatter and stay close,
It causes them to sing the most.
Sunshine, rain drops and morning dew,
Plays a part, for Guess Who, to renew.

THE DOOR BELL RANG

There stood two teenage girls,
With a baby kitty held in their arms.
We want to find a home for it,
Mom says, It's got to go, put it to sleep.
I really don't want it,
but I'll keep it till you find a home.
I called it "Cotty", the love grew.
It was a Manx, in two weeks the bell rang.
"We came to get the kitty,
we found a home for it".
To their surprise, you can't have the kitty.
I fell in love with Cotty.
She has a bed, it's own sand box, a name, Cotty.
They were speechless, so you can fall in love
With a baby.

SEPTEMBER HARVEST MOON

Animals playing round the wheat stocks.
Shadows from the moon, dancing in the meadow
dunes.
In an old dried up tree, sat a Hoot Owl
Looking for what may be.
A Rabbit brought her babies out to play.
Pumpkins were a dead give away,
September closing off, Halloween signs all about.
Getting ready to buy the treats,
And meet the kids with some treats.

SAW DUST HEART

If I had a sawdust heart,
I'd trim it up to match the part.
It's hard to jump-start a heart,
That's been crushed and hurt.
I wear a smile,
pretend from the start all the while.
So I can be in modern style.
My love was the best ever had.
I'll admit, I did flirt, it's so sad.
They say an affair that never was,
We can talk about it, like it was.
Dream about what it might have been.
My heart keeps telling me,
No sin, just lost in a dream.
Better luck next time, so it seems.

FALLING IN LOVE

When I was young I met a guy.
Fell in love, couldn't say why.
He was usually late, his excuses were great.
The good times we saw on a date.
His car was noisy, that didn't matter.
I cuddled close so my teeth didn't chatter.
Teachers training was a must,
Two more years was a plus.
I worried about little words,
As to whom it may concern.
Then again I knew what was ability,
Did have to earn.
Finally summed up 60 years of teaching.
Stacks of music, groups in the leading

PRINCE OF PEACE

Prince of Peace send our Mommies and Daddy
home.
Let them play games that are in fun.
Games that don't hurt anyone.
We read about World Peace, followed,
He will settle first,
The people with War Time Thirst.
Prince of Peace travel by speed of light,
Will visit to tell his plan.
World Peace, a World Wide Delight.
Let us all kneel and pray.
World Peace in unison tonight.
A Prayer to put things right.

A FAVORITE POEM

When you choose a poem to read,
Could you enjoy a farm scene?
Where Papa was suppose to be?
He checked the moisture in the field.
Nebraska corn, what he thought it could yield.
Watermelon's ready to market it next week.
The get togethers with neighbors and family,
you can't believe.
Yes, we played music, moonlight magic.
If we missed their favorites,
It could be almost tragic.
Memories I remember.
August 1999.

HOLD ME TIGHT

We recited our vows, that the law allows.
Please hold me tight,
I still feel the fright of the night.
Please hold me tight,
Take away the fright.
Tell me it seems so right.
The best of the heart beats, so perfect goes along.
To romance and heartbeat of our song.
The violin with heart felt love.   ·
Touches the heart strings,
With tenderness from above.
Hold me tight, it seems so right, tonight.
July 1999

BIRTHDAY

A birthday is worth a wish.
Birthdays are showered with kisses.
Number sixteen, the style, falling in love.
We play a part in motherhood.
Thank God, when we are understood.
A Grandmother, she plays with pride.
The Honor is hard to hide.
We've lived, we've lost,
We are proud to be here at any cost.

GATEWAY TO PEACE

Let happiness belong to you.
Thank the thoughts from afar.
Someone in charge of the stars,
Hangs the moon out at night.
Make sure it's just right.
Tell the birds to make a nest,
There will be babies to invest.
Account of the hairs on our heads.
Soul mates looking where, so they said;
Our greatest leaders searching,
T o avoid the pitfalls lurking.
Good thoughts carry and find a way.
To better ways, for better days.
Just look for the Gateway to Peace.

LIVE AND LEARN

When shadows grow tall and the evening is nigh.
I think of friends gone on with a sigh.
A sunset of life prepared as we strife.
Things must be better on the other side.
Hot can be cold and cold can be hot.
Tears bring memories that brought us to shame.
Laughter cried out, I'm not to blame.
Take the bitter with the sweet.
You'll survive, whatever you meet.

RIGHT AND WRONG

I listen to the right and wrong,
Answer questions as I go along.
Why does getting even seem so right,
When someone's so hurt?
They have night fright.
Even tho they bring your mail,
And picked up the empty pail.
Would you take me home from Sunday School?
So I can soak my feet in your pool.
I don't have a Grandmother or a Mom,
To have her wrap my hurts.
When I grow up to be a lady,
I'll be hugging and loving my baby.

NIGHT BIRD CRY

Listen for the night bird cry,
When you're alone on a stormy night.
Dark clouds covered the moon,
Stars are waiting to show up soon.
Coyotes howl to call their pool.
Break of dawn they'll start their school.
Herder sheep are enjoying peace.
Alert to any harms way for their fleece.
Listen for the night bird cry.
Beware there's trouble lurking close tonight.
May 1999

DON'T PASS IT UP 1999

When our time is growing short,
Think of the favors that came our way.
Let our friends be the ones to say.
You are the one that helps make my day.
Tell them your strength, give me an incentive to
pray.
Let us group in huddles to brighten our day.
We whisper our love,
And send our love.
1999

SWEET NOTHINGS

I loved the sweet nothings you promised to do.
If it happened, it would be sweeter than true.
When you skipped out, it put me in doubt.
I still knew he had time to be back,
But decided it was faith that he lacked.
It's always been said,
"There's better fish to be had,
that hasn't been caught."
It's sad; we gave up what we had, so what?
I just won the lottery, Sweet Sorrow.

ALOHA MOONLIGHT AND YOU

Roses blooming in June, Birthdays coming soon.
Some weddings are in the plans,
Beach weddings on the sands.
Hula dancing is in demand, palm trees
sway as they may.
 Leis are ready for the day,
Guitars and ukuleles ready to play.
Happy Birthday on my Wedding Day.
Hula Hula dancing and palm trees sway
On the wedding day.
Aloha, moonlight and you.

MOOD SWINGS

Mood swings last for a day,
Waiting for an answer, what to say.
I see eyes that can twinkle from blue to grey.
Maybe yes, maybe no, and that's the way it will go.
I've shinned my shoes, cut my hair.
She wears false rats in hers.
I'm not suppose to know.
Mood Swings come and go.
Now I've walked in the mud and let my hair grow,
In my Mood Swing. I found the answer.
My answer is "No."
March 1999

IF YOU COULD BE

If you could be, what would you be?
I'd be a leprechaun, stand at a door
To know what goes on.
I'd hate to wear those stupid shoes.
Turned up at the toes, where could you go?
Or what could you do?
If you danced an Irish jig---
It would cause you to lose your wig.
Top of the morning, I'd say, as you pass by.
I'll see you later by and by,
And listen for a night bird cry.

KARMA

K. is for Kindness
    We endeavor to enjoy
A. Always comes our way
    In need of employ.
R. Could be a romance
    We neglect from time to time
M. Is for many, many times
    Our loved one we choose to neglect
A. Always Count your
    Blessing one by one
    They will stay with you
    Second to None.

HEART THROB

I'd like a heart throb, that would
Jump start my heart.
I've slowed down my wants,
Would a jump start play a part?
My body's drooping, and I love to eat.
A new heart throb would make me want to look
neat.
I could take a trip around the mall,
Wear high heeled shoes so I'll look tall.
A new heart throb would solve it all.
March 1999

I'M IN THE NOW

Memories turn to ashes, aches turn to dust.
Thoughts can be a pleasure,
Or lost in a fog of dust.
As we count our decades, recollect the past,
Our knowledge is so precious, at last,
Just to know how progress has grown.
Some homes in my life didn't have a phone.
You couldn't have a secret, the neighbors listened in.
If you talked about her latest beau,
Just remember, don't say Joe!
We harvested ice, made houses out of straw.
July fourth celebration, fried chicken, ice cream,
Mamma's delicious cake to take.
Buck board wagons, beds were made.
The Home Town Band serenade made the day.

TWO OLD ROCKERS

Two old rockers rocking along.
Grandma knitting for the family throng.
Grandpa humming a song, a winter wonderland.
Changing the scenes, while Mom checked
The kitchen for holiday treats.
Dad waxed the skis, when he hit the breeze.
The sleighs all painted, one marked for sale.
They must be new and pretty too.
Ready to hit the trail.
The 2000 Family.

DON'T PLAY GAMES

Don't play games with your heart.
When love comes along, maybe it's time to listen.
Could it be in a song?
Check the things you're missin'
Don't play games with your heart.
When a titillating heart says, play the part.
Love can come and go,
If it's right you will know.
Don't play games with you heart.
If a titillating heart says
"Play your Part."

I WRITE THE MUSIC

I write the music to enlighten my heart.
The memories so strewed are so dim to keep us
apart.
One time the flame aimed at your heart,
So tender and right could jump start my heart.
Let us find who's to blame, a wasted love is a
shame.
I dream of wedding chimes,
Could it be in our dreams come true, in our time.

I JUST GOT THE NEWS

No more sugar if you want to lose weight.
You can eat the ice without the cream.
A T-Bone Steak stays in your dreams,
Even sour dough is bad, that even makes me sad.
When I think of corn, I sob now,
I just boil the buttered cob.
If you come for supper, you can bet I'll hide the
butter.
If you think I'm on the up and up,
I suppose you think I'm a cover up.
Think what you may, there'll come a day.
It takes grit and I don't have it.

START THE DAY

Start the day and say, come what may.
Pretend we are sent a great day.
Think good thoughts until ten o'clock.
From then on listen for good luck to knock.
Maybe you've won a free lunch.
Maybe you're invited to go with the bunch.
Don't get down hearted, Aunties in town.
Now you'll be asked to show her around.
There's always a way, if there's another day.

STAY ON LINE

Stay on line, be on time, keep your word, stay alive.
Smile away your tears, you can erase the lines of years.
Candle light is kind at night,
Frequent the place to be polite.
If you sit alone at home, check the black book phone.
Honey, should I say I'm alone,
Baby, you've been gone so long.
It was time to ring a gong.
Just stay on line, be on time, keep your word, stay alive.

1998 BABY

A baby sent from heaven in nineteen ninety eight.
Received a royal welcome.
No restrictions or complaints.
She looked the family over,
decided she landed in clover.
Excitement and love fills the home.
Renewed the future thoughts of love.
An Angel tipped a wing from above.
She visited me at Christmas time,
When she brought a Christmas Chime.
In my heart I needed in my time,
Madison Marie to cheer me.
I called her M and M candy.

NINETEEN NINETY NINE

Nineteen Ninety Nine has taken it's place in time.
It tells us it's inclined to rhyme.
A glow of power dancing above.
A respect and honor we love.
Now when the trumpet's on alert,
The rumors of war brings a hurt.
Let our prayers join in force.
May we study the general course.
We are told to get back on track.
Bless our safety and our homes.
Don't fall in love with life time loans.
Let us look for peace of mind.
We'll find life, God's loving and kindness.

HAPPY NEW YEAR

Our World of Wonders for 1999, causes us to ask,
Will we settle our wayward ways?
Yes, the end of 1998 at last,
Let us look forward to new ways.
We cherish our long time friends.
We will, no doubt, find new worries in line.
Waiting to meet the challenges, excitement in mind.
A new hobby could help us find,
new thoughts in place of old.
The end of the Rainbow of Gold,
Blessings in 1999.

LOVE IS LIKE A FUNGUS

Should I leave before you ask me?
When our love is becoming weak.
Let's talk about the in between.
Our love is so great, it seems.
Don't listen to rumors,
Just uttered in discreet.
A love is like a fungus,
replaced to normal over night.
Talk it over, listen to the tender voice,
He loves us.
Love is like a fungus, pops up over night.
Pop Corn rhythm, Truly God given.

JOHN GLENN

Thirty six years ago, I waited with baited breath.
I wanted him to find Heaven,
It surely must be God given.
My heart beating triple, today in 1998, a slower rate.
John Glenn, still game to go,
He is from Ohio, you might know.
Everything's fine so far.
USA, stand around and cheer.
Prayers for family, where ever you are.
Glenn said, "I'm better at 77,
 than some were ever given."
This will benefit aging.
4600 miles per hour, gets me.
Off they went without a nitch,
We will wait for their return.
Nope, they're paid for what they earn.

Written October 28, 1998 at 10;00am
By Alice Hartley, age 91 years.

WHEN WORLD PEACE ARRIVES

Life will have a better meaning,
When World Peace arrives.
Turn evil hind side too,
Let Our Maker become alive.
Send for love in bundles,
watch the War and Hate tumbles.
Replace it with a kind of reasoning.
The sun will rise in pleasing.
Let the sun shine in the shadows.
If this sounds like niney niney,
There can be a new beginning.
Put up slogans, Praise our Leaders.
Peace, understanding in the taking.

WHO

Who, sprinkled the stars for everyone to see?
Who, takes care of the moon, to where it may be?
Who, changes the seasons, for different reasons?
Who, sends their love to comfort us?
Who, brings the reason for family trust?
Who, starts the day, find our pleasure to make our day?
Who, do we claim for our very own to show us the way?
Our Maker is here to stay, come what may!
June 17, 1999.

THE VOICE OF MUSIC

The voice of music comes from within.
The touch you render,
The spirit next to your heart.
Made with ambles so tender.
Make it speak of love,
Or a spirit from above.
A memory brought to mind.
A secret in our lives of a kind.
We mention not the hurts that die,
But the times we enlighten to be wise.
Oh, how often we're ready to decide.
Even tho you might surmise.
A heart felt love, time felt so wise.

I CRIED MY HEART OUT

You said you were leaving, no need to grieve.
We would be better as I see,
There's sunshine no matter where.
There'll be someone waiting to care.
I did love you, I can't deny.
Now I can't remember why.
You go your way, I'll go mine.
It's always exciting to look and find.
I've thought it over, I want you by my side.
I love you by my side.

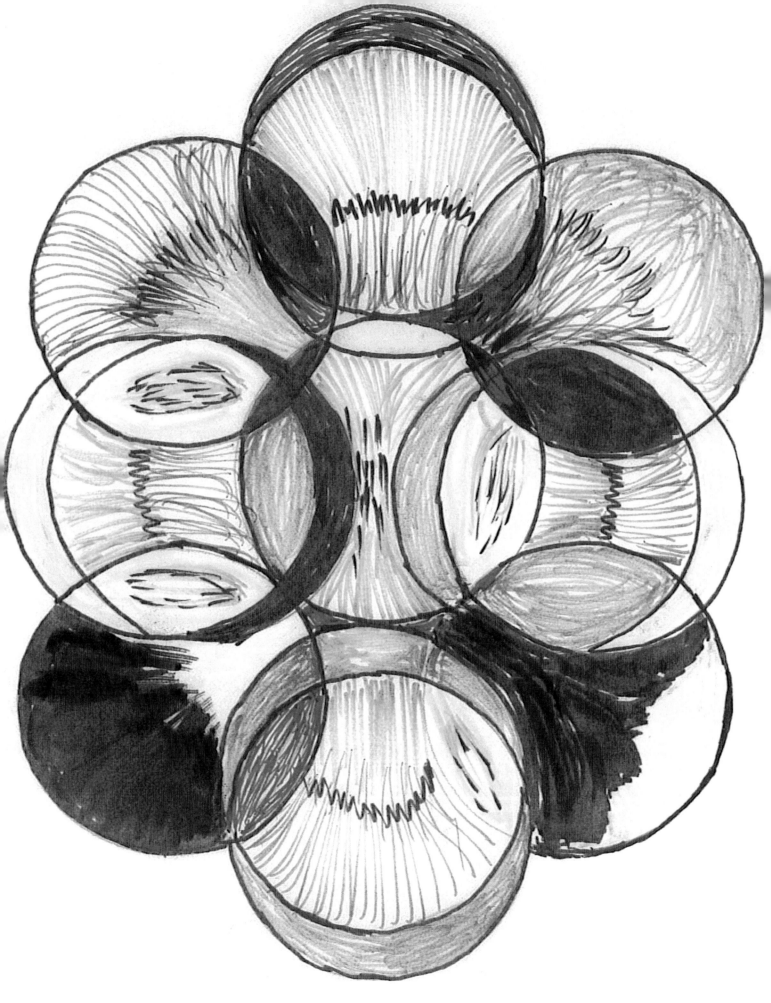

GOLDEN MEMORIES

Years gone by, braided hair with ribbons,
Always in supply.
Sun Bonnet Sue, Grandma made new.
We collected wild berries and enjoyed the
cherries.
Hot cakes and choke cherry jelly.
The enjoyable get together rally.
Winter meant, saw up ice, pack it away.
Summertime Ice Cream, was a treat for the day.
Camp fires down at the old home made pond.
We never forgot when Christmas came along.
We picked out the tree and knew it would be,
Trimmed with holly and gifts, and names for even
me!

IT SEEMS SO RIGHT

It seems so right to have someone to love.
With a home to have toys to pick up.
Little clothes to laundry and hang up.
Kisses waiting for Daddy,
When he comes home each day.
Smelly kitchen for the daddy's hugs.
Mom is welcoming him for the day.
It seems so right, A family prayer at night.
And ask to start tomorrow with a brighter day.
July 1999

REMEMBERING

Remembering starlight magic,
As we strolled 'neath the mellow moon.
There was a path, yes, logic,
To dream, to revise a knowledge.
Seems could be so near, true.
War clouds rumbled above us.
Could break our dreams in two.
Have faith in our hearts,
Let prayers take a part, Peace on it's way.
Peace on Earth to stay.

POETRY LIVES ON FOREVER

I express myself as to say,
To friend and loved ones each day.
We let them know what we are thinking of,
And renew the by-gone days.
Memories are so special in many ways.
A poem can be yellow with age,
But so modern, even today.
We mend it, we save it.
Old books are full of it.
Treasures so dear to one's heart,
And until death do we part.

2000 DREAMING

It was a dream,
I was dancing with a shadow on the moon.
Our feet light and fancy too.
We danced fantastically,
Dipped and swayed to a magic tune.
He whispered , I'm suppose to go to planet Earth.
The stars will shine soon, to keep me in line.
Dreams will be real, things will appeal.
I'll bring you back home for mine.
Oh, what a time.

BURDEN IN OUR HEART

If you carry a burden in your heart,
Ask God to release it.
We are God's helpers.
If we don't, He is helpless.
Tell him you are helpless with out his care.
He will answer you, I swear.
Praise Him for the sunshine,
And for the skies of blue.
If you will only listen,
He will praise you, too.
Count the pedals on the daisies.
Make a wish, say "hello,"
He will listen to your wishes.
Be happy to know.

WHEN YOU LAY ME DOWN TO REST

When you lay me down to rest,
Wear a smile instead of tears.
Think of all pitfalls I tried to meet.
With all my strength thru out the years.

As you reminisce my variegated life,
You will have to admit, I met strife,
And treated it just as part of life.
A passing faze could only be,
The way to better things I need.

I had a dream right from the start.
What I wanted would come my way.
Music was imbedded in my heart.
It grew and grew with fulfillment,
You would have to say.

One's success starts with you.
First is a thought, construct the way to go.
Think not of the wealth you'll gain,
But your way of life enrichment.
For the betterment of your fellowmen.
It will bring sunshine to you day to day.
May 1995

JUNE 1998

Paint the Town will touch up my home again this year.
My deck in the back will get a face lift.
{Oh, does it need it}
I've met such nice people checking
on the spruce up duties.
We should praise our Boise town,
Volunteers and helpers.
No wonder our town is "special" named,
"Beautiful Boise Town".
I'm going to Thank them in advance.
I'm a Senior, and take the opportunity to say,
A big "Thank You" for all the beauty everyone
Brings to Boise.

CARD MAKING HOBBY

I make greeting cards and still wonder.
I've been reminded it is cheaper.
They are time consuming, to say the least.
When they say they are a keeper,
My heart beats with pride and try harder.
Even take more time to make them neater.
I paint hearts and flowers, even birds.
I picture the birds singing my words.

SUN OF A GUN

Sun of a Gun, I'm ninety one.
I've lived and loved a life home spun.
Studied positive and negative, like a river runs.
Doodads and fads, I followed some.
I analyzed the results from beginning to end.
I was told to be skeptical but would probably win.
I wrote songs and poems too, studied music to no end.
I listened to the melodies of birds in early spring.
Now my cup of hot coffee awaits for day to begin.
I listen for a shut-in to make my telephone to ring.
It makes my day, they can barely hear me say,
What's new?
I still love good food, cook and serve, play music too.
1998

LET ME BE A NEED TO THEE

When the time comes to climb the golden stairs.
I'll be content to dust all the way up to tell
about my wares.
My first statement will be, I'm not a joiner,
But I'm happy to be here, Your Honor.
Then a voice said; "I know you, I remember you."
You respected others in their trials and cares.
You encouraged betterment,
mediocre was never a settlement.
You looked for the best in people.
Encouraged their talents to be reapable.
Toil, to you, was a privilege indeed.
Accomplishment is your dire need.
Now I ask; "Let me be a need to thee."
September 10, 1995

CLEANSING OF THE HEART

A heart that is cluttered, with changing of times,
Sometimes is smothered with no reasons and
rhymes.
What seems so right in my yesterdays,
Seems so wrong in modern ways.
No time set aside for self pride.
Some time, wasted time, we like to hide.
"God says" the sunshine is here to stay.
Let your spirits light the way.
Joy, can be the mistle of the trees, and the
refreshment
Of the breeze.
Mother Earth is waiting to produce indeed,
Just a few plants and seeds is all she needs.
Hands that toil with the soil, is God's way after all.
Gardening will bring you contentment,
enrichment
And cleansing of the heart.
September 9, 1995.

JUNE 15, 1996

When you reach the age of 89, you begin to think
About the time, Yes, it's getting towards the sun set.
It's amazing how the joys of sunset colors are yet.
I enjoy the flowers that come and go.
Yes, they have at times, they seem to know.
We're like the flowers that fade away.
They seem to know they will come again some day.
To replace, with the beauty, as good as new.
Even the plants dry and rot, their strength will
furnish
Help for the next crop.
As I look at the stars that twinkle at night.
Oh, how thrilling it would be to be free to mingle
Among the galaxies.
We can read, dream, and wonder.
We've read, so the bible says;
"We know not from where we cometh,
We know not where we goeth."
The secret of contentment is: " Trust in our Maker."
With peace in our hearts, nothing could be
greater.

SOME DAY

Some day you'll want me to want you.
Some day, you will know the need of me.
Some day, my name could be fading away.
New nests can play a part to say.
Faded in my jealous, jealous heart.
Time can bring lonely times, so precious,
So memorable to part.
Bring back the days of wonderment.
Turn back the clock of need.
God knows my heart is aching.
When he took the privilege of taking,
My love, my future away.
Lord I'm coming home.
March 12, 1999

LOOKING FOR THE KEY TO HEAVEN

Looking for the key to heaven,
When you can find it in your heart.
Tucked beneath the blessing, we forgot thy part.
Sunshine warms the flowers and kisses off the dew.
It can warm our heart if we think it through.
Clouds that gather and sprinkle rain
and visit the flowers, before time to complain.
This is God's way of saying, I'll not forsake thee.
Listen to the music playing, I'm calling you
home.
March 14, 1999

MARK, MEL AND BABY

So near as I can tell, Mel, Mark and baby.
So just like the doctor ordered.
Her hair is black and eyes to match.
Color conscious alert, that's the fact.
I saw a dimple peak thru.
Even Grandpa Loren, noticed it too.
Mamma Mel, with reserved comments to tell.
Daddy Markus, so proud, chimed like a dinner
bell.
I must confess, I'm impressed.
Prettiest, sweetest, even liked my music.
Made my day, quickened my heart beat, I confess.

LIFE

Sometimes we are tossed like a cork on an
angry sea,
Sometimes our lives are calm and tranquil as can be.
Sometimes we are teased with the bitter and the
sweet.
Sometimes we are given a path to follow that seems
So complete.
Sometimes we ignore the warning signs.
Who are we to have to be reminded
of the changing times.
Sometimes we won't ask for help,
just go stumbling along.
Until we stub our toe.
We are like a wounded dove, that falls to the ground.
Finely we know what's missing,
Is God's unconditional Love.
September 5, 1993

CHOICE

God gives us a choice, we can be pleasant,
We can be free, to enjoy our God given freedom.
No matter, if only in thought to scheme and think.
The rains in our life can dampen our spirits.
When the sun comes back we are aware of our
merits.
If we look for perfection, we can find flaws.
Even God's way can cause us to pause.
He's given the storms, even their choice,
To wash and ruin the path of their ploys.
Then comes the rivers so angry and wild.
How could it run for years so gentle and mild?
Does God feel so desperate, he has to explode?
One could guess he carries an excess load.
Do we help to comfort Him,
or is it just our selfish ways.
We count ourselves, Christians,
We're borne again Spirit, we say.
When things are black and storms at hand,
Can we still be God's helpers and answer to his
commands? Just asking.
July 23, 1993.

UNSATISFIED

As we are put on Earth, everyone is "Special"
In their rights and worth.
Every color of skin has a beauty.
Black stands the heat of the sun.
Dark up to different shades,
Identifies us to our heritage from where we came.

Hair used to be our shining glory.
Tresses we combed and caressed each morning.
We've arrived to the time they'll say,
"I don't like mine."
Change the color, change the style.
Just want to look different all the while.
We've got yellow, purple, blue and green.
On each head, five colors to be seen.
Let it hang in the eyes, fly past the food.
Cut out messages to attract the cool.
Straighten the curls and curl the straight.
It's making them nervous and even hate.

We are trying to get ready for outer space.
We forget to "Thank God" in this horrid haste.
It's getting scary to even think of how we look.
We expect a miracle of the teachers today,
Without applying in any way.
Self study is out of style, let's take a note from
Lincoln.
Self made people can still be worthwhile.
Set your goal, make up your mind,
Determination, wear a smile and you'll gain every
time.
I've been down the trail.
September 12, 1993.

The one you lost had love to last.
His life was filled with thoughtfulness, kindness.
May each have a special way of life,
Even tho it's a plant or a tree.
July 26, 1993.

IT'S GOSSIP

I'd love to tell somebody about something new.
I'm lonesome and bored, I'm plain lonesome to
see you.
We could talk about cookies, Aunt Lizy said
"Aunt Annie baked for me." The mix was old,
Couldn't read the instructions, crumbled in the
fold.
I told her bring it anyway.
I'm going to be serving refreshments next month,
On get together day.
I hear it's bad to gossip, can even be called a sin.
Why meet your friends, if I don't have news to spin?
I'll talk about my aches and pains,
I've had experience to complain.
Join a group to gossip, it's a perfect place to
catch up.
September 1998.

THE HOME BOUND SHIP

The sun is sinking in the west.
The wayward winds at rest, on the crest.
The home bound ship winning it's way home.
Our soldiers are returning to sweethearts left alone.
The U.S. Flag is flying from the bough.
The ones on the shore are waving, ship ahoy.
The home town band waiting for the baton
command.
God Bless America and for what it stands.
The reunion sprinkled with tears and joy.
Some are missing, we must admit.
War was never won without regret.
1998.

GUM

I love you Granny, deed I do.
I've got gum on my shoe, same as you.
I don't know what to do, it is stuck just like glue.
I know you have troubles too.
What I'd like to know, "what's new"
If I walked on grandma's rug, just to give her a hug,
It would be a no, no, no!
I have love that goes beyond, I have love to spare,
You know.
I'll be glad to mow the lawn, take an I.O.U. for
later on.
Love you Granny and Pappy, deed I do.

LET US STAY IN LOVE

We ask our maker from above, let us stay in love.
We recited our vows and took out our bows.
Prayed we could stay in love.
Told my doubter, to take a walk.
We don't listen to idle talk.
We stay together as time goes by.
Short comings forgiven, the reason why.
We live to love, love to live.
Respect and kindness is what we give.
We ask our Maker from above, Let us stay in
Love.

BOO HOO BOO HOO

Everything is dunky dory, when love is on it's way.
They will say they never loved before,
And their love is here to stay.
It sounds so sweet when they call my name,
And say, you are just a dream.
They can say, you are so wonderful.
My world doesn't seem the same.
Then he comes up missing,
Where he's at, I haven't a clue, nothing left to do.
Just Boo Hoo, Boo Hoo and look for someone new.
W.W. dot com, Where are you?

ONE IN MILLIONS

One in millions will win a chance of a lifetime.
Just accept you chances are slim.
Send it in, get in the swim.
The mail stacks like a compost pile.
Keep it to raise veggies or stay in style.
Dream of what you might win in time.
Even if Grandpa falls asleep when you begin.
Ask the dowser from time to time.
Argue if it says, "not a dime."
Time is close, it keeps me alive.
Now it's past, I must say "Jive."
Say what you will, my gifts are nil.
Guess I'll just pan for gold in Idaho.
P.S. Remember there is Fool's Gold too!

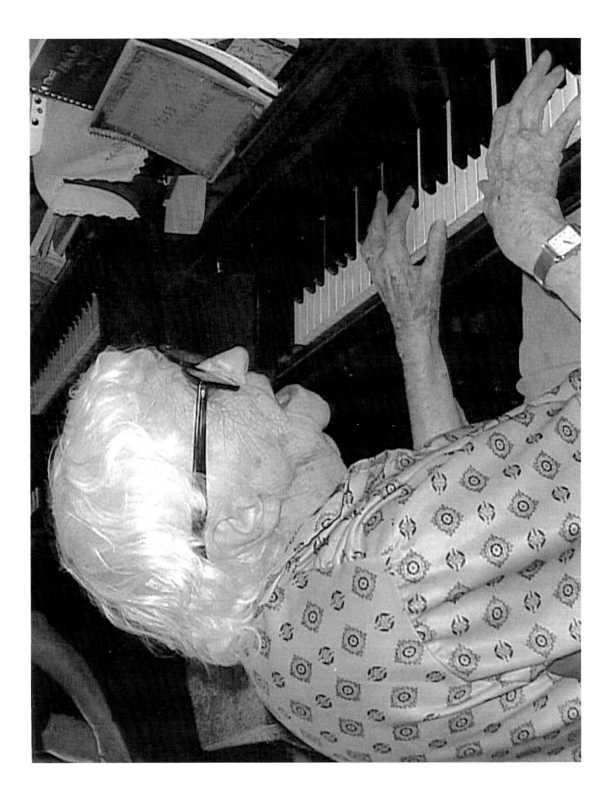

LANGUAGE OF EXPERIENCE

The language of experience is put together
with pro and con.
With a two way street we travel on,
still looking for a magic wand---
The pattern of one's lifestyle is visited
with uncertainty from time to time---
Which enchants and strengths for embetterment
to come alive---
Age is beautiful, it expels knowledge,
the responsibility of becoming parents
Preparing and watching the action swing
with helpless orders of head---
It's reality so as to resemble our liberal past---
Our first thoughts will be, will they ever grow up,
and can I last--
I spoke up aloud, all most frightened,
saying I grew up and took the lessons and bumps
My life wasn't all trumps, while my parents aged
and turned grey---
We must travel a path of intensity and stress
Face reality, it's a way of life, take the test,
even tho it doesn't turn out the best.

Frank O. Henrikson

ABOUT THE AUTHOR

When June 15, 1995 arrives, if God willing, I'll be 88 years old. It's amusing to meet different ages. The young are sometimes told about elderly people or senile. They wonder what do we remember, can we cope with modern times? When I was young and visited an eighty year old person, I told them good-by---Thinking it was over soon and I may not get to see them again. But you can be much older coping with every day. Still writing books, poetry, sewing, building, gardening, even pleasant to talk with. We want to be wanted and needed. We can call shut-ins, to cheer them, cook a special meal now and then. We can't swing family dinners any more, make a cake or a pie. I love to watch style shows and study them in the magazines. Then I think, Oh my, I dressed as a flapper when I was a teenager, floppy hats, short skirts made on the bias. They flipped when we walked and showed our garters. Yes, we've all gone through a teenage stage. When we've mastered that, we thought we had it made. Little did we know.